EDIBLE WILD

PLANTS FORAGING

FOR BEGINNERS

**Learn How to Identify Safely and
Harvest Nature's Green Gifts
in the Pacific Northwest, Midwest,
and Southeast Territories**

CONTENTS

INTRODUCTION

There is a certain level of primeval satisfaction when you are able to successfully forage for berries, herbs and other edible plants in the woods. You may have purchased this book with the intent to learn more about how to properly forage in the woods and fields around you for the sustainable produce that nature has provided. While there is certainly a vast amount of greenery from which you could make your choices, not all plants are edible and if you are unguided as to how to properly tell apart edible from inedible plants, you may find yourself in a pickle. Some plants are truly edible, while others have parts that are edible while the other parts may be toxic to consume. This book serves to be a guide by which you will be able to safely forage for sustainable and ecologically friendly produce and live off the land successfully. You would be able to save on grocery bills since you would be able to source your produce from nature itself.

chokeberry

cherry

hawthorn

bilberry

cloudberry

raspberry

strawberry

bird cherry

blackberry

Chapter 1

AT THE ROOT OF IT ALL

1.1 THE HISTORY OF EDIBLE PLANTS

Prior to the evolution of humanity into an agrarian society, the earliest human civilizations survived as hunter-gatherers. These were the people who were able to live off the land, and once the resources in the land petered out, they moved on to more fruitful areas. Despite the presence of predators that could easily overpower the humans back then as their main competition, and the weather conditions that prevented fruitful harvests, humanity was able to survive and flourish through the act of foraging. The ability to forage for edible plants back then was crucial, in that the earliest humans needed to know when was the best time to harvest certain types of plants, and this was carried on even with the development of the agrarian society that allowed for the cultivation of these wild plants into a regular supply of food that would enable them to survive winter.

Given that hunter-gatherers do have the connotation that they are primarily carnivores, this idea would be erroneous. Take for example Native American societies, which are hunter-gatherers in classification, but an observation of their dietary practices indicate that they utilized a plant-based diet. One characteristic that the Native American population shares with other indigenous peoples throughout the world is that they do have the necessary knowledge to differentiate edible

wild plants from those plants that are unfit for human consumption. The Native American tribes were able to supplement the protein sources that they had with the edible wild plants that were abundant in their respective tribal lands. What may be just a random thicket of greenery to our untrained eyes may be the food source for a group of people, so it would be best to be careful with how we treat plants.

The responsibility to gather and differentiate edible plants was accorded to the women and children. A usual image that comes to mind is that the men are out in the fields, stalking their prey; while the women and children remained near their tents, and foraged in the nearby fields for the plants, herbs, seeds and nuts that they use to augment their meals. It is expected that the consumption of food varied in accordance with the seasons. Food stores on the first day of spring were rapidly consumed to compensate for the lack of food throughout the winter. This practice was cyclical in nature, in that once their hunger was sated, these hunter-gatherers began to forage to replenish their depleted food stores in preparation for the coming winter. While most of the produce were consumed in their fresh state, or were immediately prepared into food; extra produce was preserved through traditional means to form part of their winter food supplies. Hunter-gatherers often dried food and combined with other types of food to form food items that would be suitable for prolonged storage such as pemmican.

The Native American tribes populated throughout the North American continent had their own customary diets that were composed of plants and other wildlife native to their areas. They were able to live off the land for centuries with the use of basic foraging tools. These tools included sharpened sticks and crude knives that could be used to dig up root crops; and hand-woven baskets and pouches to carry the foraged plants back to their camps for preparation by the women of the tribe. If one would recall the life of the Pilgrims when they first landed in North America with their favored crops, they were able to survive the North American winters with the supplementation of other edible wild plants back then such as corn, squash and beans. Of course, these latter three are by no means considered wild in this contemporary age, but given that the North American climate was too cold for traditional European crops to grow, these edible wild plants enabled these Pilgrims and other colonists to survive and make a life in North America.

1.2 WHAT MAKES A WILD PLANT EDIBLE?

In the previous paragraph, plants that were considered wild such as corn, beans and squash became instrumental to the survival of the early colonists, and thus were cultivated to such a degree that they were no longer considered as wild. This begs the question: What makes an Edible Wild Plant?

To define this, it would be necessary to break the phrase up into its components. At this point, we already know what a plant is thanks to our science classes. We each have different ideas on what makes a plant edible and what makes a plant wild. Collectively, Edible Wild Plants are plants that have not undergone any type of modification such as Genetic Modification, nor have they been specially crossbred with other species to ensure that the plant produced carries the most desirable characteristics of both species. These plants are also composed of a one or more parts that are fit for human consumption once these parts have been gathered at a certain stage of their development and if they have been properly prepared and cooked.

What does the latter part mean? Just because you are able to eat the product of one plant does not necessarily mean that the rest of the plant is edible. You may be able to enjoy the tomato for instance, but under no circumstances are you permitted to eat the flowers of the tomato, nor its relatives such as the eggplant and the potato whose flowers are equally as toxic as the tomato. Plants have parts that are certainly edible, be it the roots, stems, leaves, berries, or flowers. There are also plants whose structures are too woody to eat, plants whose other parts are used as medicine rather than food, and parts that are simply too unpalatable for the human taste. It becomes necessary to identify not only the wild plants that are edible, but the specific parts of the wild plant that are edible for us to eat. A good rule of thumb is, if in doubt, throw it out. It would be better to spend a few dollars on a grocery bill rather than spend thousands on a hospital bill, more so in this economy.

Earlier, it was mentioned that not only do you have to gather the right parts of the plant for food, but also gather them at the right stage of development. As with the other parts of the plant, some parts of the plant, once they have matured, become toxic or unpalatable, hence it is necessary to equip yourself with the knowledge of not only knowing what to gather, but when to gather it. One of the plants in this list is the common Milkweed, which can produce pods with immature seeds that are edible while still at that stage and are suitable for culinary usage. Once these same

pods reach maturity however, they become poisonous and this poison cannot be removed from the plant no matter which culinary preparation it is used in. Throughout this book then, it would be necessary to note the part of the plant that is edible, and at which stage is this plant safe to eat.

Lastly, it would be necessary to determine the proper way to prepare a plant for consumption. There are parts of a plant that are edible only after they have been processed or prepared in a certain way to reduce their unpalatable qualities. For instance, some people find the texture of okra to be off-putting due to the slimy texture that it exudes, but appreciate it once it has been cooked into a stew, or if it has been fried to reduce the sliminess associated with it. This is just one way to properly process a food. Some edible wild plants need more stringent forms of preparation such as the removal of seeds from the fruit of a plant; the removal of water-soluble substances from a plant through leaching, or simply the application of heat at specific temperatures to ensure the plant becomes more edible. Dandelion, another edible wild plant contains substances that can induce diarrhea and excessive urination if left unprocessed, but when boiled, these effects are significantly reduced. Again, it is necessary to know the part of the plant that should be used, and when the said part remains fit to eat.

1.3 THE EDIBLE WILD PLANT OPTION

At this point, you probably feel intimidated by the amount of detail that you need to familiarize yourself with. You might even ask yourself, would a grocery trip be a more worthwhile use of time? All you have to do there is pick and sniff, choose and weigh and you're done with your grocery trip, all without the need to traipse through fields and subject yourself to insects and the heat of the sun. This is an option mind you, but there are a variety of reasons as to why people prefer to forage for their produce rather than to purchase their greens from the grocery,

A more logical reason as to why people forage is for economic purposes. This is a more relatable idea since with the rise in grocery items, you might consider foraging to be a more economical way to save your money, especially since it is sourced freely from your forests and fields. Other people simply forage to add more variety to their diet other than cultivated greens. A bowl of romaine lettuce might hold lesser appeal than wild varieties of lettuce that you do not have to pay any price at all. Other reasons for the use of edible wild plants include the need to commune with nature itself, or to sate your curiosity now that local restaurants have joined in the locavore movement. The latter statement means that restaurants now pay attention to the use of local, sustainable

ingredients in their dishes rather than have their produce shipped from other parts of the country – which drive up the prices of the food that is served in these restaurants.

A more biologic reason is that, because wild plants are not cultivated, their flavors are more concentrated, and thus make great additions to a variety of dishes. Because of their wild state, they also have a higher concentration of nutrition and have more vitamins and minerals compared to cultivated varieties of produce. Spinach is widely known to be an iron-rich food, however, because of the presence of oxalic acid in the plant, the body is unlikely to absorb a lot of iron from it. Spinach is less nutritionally dense compared to the consumption of plants like chickweed and dandelion which carry more iron content than spinach itself.

There is also the matter of survival in reference to the consumption and identification of edible wild plants. We have heard stories of people who found themselves marooned in certain areas without a food supply who then died of starvation. It would be advantageous on your part to have the necessary knowledge to know which plants you could safely consume should you find yourself in this event, rather than subject yourself to starvation or poison when you consume an unfamiliar plant in the hopes to stave off starvation. This knowledge is useful regardless of the type of climate you find yourself in. Remember that Native Americans were able to thrive in a variety of climates with the edible plants that grow there, and subsequently, you would be able to find edible plants regardless of the type of climate that you find yourself in.

To be a forager, you do not need to memorize every single word that is written in this book. If you wish to do so, then that is entirely up to you. What is important is that you are able to derive the knowledge on what plant to look for, where you would be able to find the plant, the best way to gather the edible parts of the plant and the best means to prepare the plant. Again, it is important that attention be given to the stage of development of the plant, and the edible parts to assure yourself that you would not be poisoned or give yourself indigestion.

1.4 THE BIOLOGY OF EDIBLE WILD PLANTS

What is the distinction between a plant, a flower and a weed? This is a question best posed to a botanist as these are very distinct characteristics. What may be a weed to one person is a plant to another. It would be best to recall the historical aspects of the plants that we purchase from the grocery, such as lettuce, corn and tomatoes. These plants before they have been cultivated into

their more familiar iterations were wild. At some point in their development, all of these plants have developed flowers which become the fruits and vegetables that we consume. When a plant is not cultivated to maintain its appearance, it begins to resemble a weed. Simply leave the plant to grow without any intervention and it will begin to develop a structure that would bear a closer resemblance to a weed than a plant.

What does this mean for the cultivated plant? Simply that it shares the same origins with its wild ancestors if left to grown on its own. This means that edible wild plants can be food to one person and a weed to another despite the similarities in their biology. The dandelion for instance is considered a weed by many, yet in this book, it is one of the edible wild plants that warrant a second look due to the nutritional qualities it possesses. But we only scratched the surface with these. The edible parts of the plants may also include the specialized structures buried beneath the plant. The edible parts of the potatoes are the modified tubers of the potato plant, while the rest of the plant is poisonous. The carrot itself is a modified taproot, although the tops themselves make a great vegetable. But at the heart of it all, we are familiar with the brown ovals and the orange roots, but we rarely pay attention to the other parts of these familiar vegetables. Who is to say that we do not walk past a more nutritionally dense equivalent of these plants on a daily basis?

Earlier we touched upon the parts of the plant that are usually considered as edible, and how important it was to pay attention to when the plant should be harvested, how the plant should be harvested, and at what stage of development may the plant part be considered edible. This may sound a bit like science class, but, there are several parts of a plant that you may consider when you forage for the edible wild plants. These are:

» The Roots which are the parts that keep the plant attached to the soil, and help the plant absorb water and nutrients from the soil. Roots can be modified to become tubers and taproots to promote storage of nutrients and increase absorption of water from the soil.

» The stems can be herbaceous (soft) or woody in character, and are used to support the rest of the structures of the plant. Some stems such as those of rhubarb, and asparagus are edible.

» Leaves are the parts of the plant that help it undergo photosynthesis that it may produce its own food. Many leaves of the plants form the edible parts of the plant.

» The Flowers are mainly used for the reproduction of the plant, and once pollinated, they often mature to become the fruit of the plant that we eventually harvest for our consumption.

» Fruits are essentially the matured ovaries of a fertilized flower, which surround the seeds of the plant and help protect it. Some fruits may not be edible when matured, while some are not edible while they are immature. Be sure to consult the plant guide in this book to properly confirm when a fruit is considered edible.

» Seeds are contained within the fruit and are a result of fertilization of the flowers. They simply help the plant reproduce, though some seeds, like sunflower seeds and squash seeds may be cooked as a vegetable to add protein to your diet.

1.5 CONCLUSION

Throughout Chapter 1, we touched upon the importance of foraging in the evolution and survival of humanity and how it continues to retain the function today. The pages of these book are designed to help you make the best of what nature provides and allow you to identify the plants that would help supplement your diet and how to best use these plants so you can take advantage of their nutritional values.

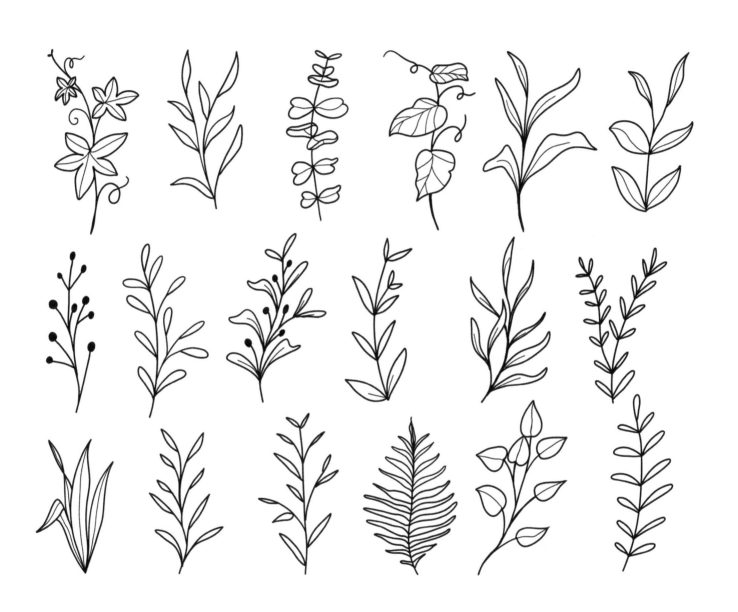

Chapter 2

THE FOUNDATIONS
OF FORAGING

Earlier in Chapter 1, we have discussed about the role of foraging in the survival of humanity and how it contributed to the progression from a hunter-gatherer society to that of an agrarian society. This later on led to the development of settlements and civilizations that evolved into our modern day cities. Now that we have emphasized the usefulness of the skill even in modern times, it would be best now to learn how to properly forage. We simply do not waltz into a forest and start picking out random greenery in the hopes that these are fit for human use, we need to build-up our knowledge of the edible plants that we may properly forage and locate the right species. This chapter will guide you on how to properly forage, regardless of the type of climate you live in.

2.1 THE PROPER IDENTIFICATION OF EDIBLE PLANTS

You do not need to glance into a forest to know that throughout North America, there are a thousand variety of plants in your locale alone. You may not even know how many of these plants are considered edible. Apart from the edible wild plants, there are those with unpalatable qualities such as too slimy or too bitter; and some that are just poisonous. Because of the potential for harm when you ingest the wrong plant, it is best to build up your knowledge on how to identify the plants that you will be able to safely consume. This book, like other books and guides will contain

pictures of the plants that would make it easier for you to familiarize yourself with. With the help of a high resolution camera, you can take a picture of the plant that you believe is edible and compare it with the pictures that are on this guide to confirm that the plant that you took a picture of is the same one in this book. Be sure to cross check with other similar looking plants to ensure that you are certain that the plant is edible.

You can narrow down the search for the edible plants through the use of filtered search terms that include the color of the flowers, the number of petals that each flower of the plant has, the shape of the leaves and the color, and the number of the leaves arranged on each stem or branch of the plant. A good idea would be to narrow down the geographical range of the plant, which is among the information listed under each plant in this book. When you are able to cross-reference the image of the plant that you have taken with its location, you would be able to ascertain that the plant is a member of the species deemed edible. This process may sound quite tedious when you read about it, but it would be wise to be extra cautious and ensure that the plant is edible and poison-free rather than regret the hastiness with a large hospital bill.

A great help to identify edible plants would be to seek the aid of an experienced forager in your area, as they would have the necessary knowledge and experience to help you identify the plants in your locale that are edible. Foragers are usually happy to pass on their knowledge and share their secrets on how to identify plants that are edible in your area. They often have a deep respect for nature and are quite passionate about the use of wild plants for culinary purposes. If there are no such foragers in your area, a good option would be to search for a Native Plant Society with a chapter that is in your area, or as close to it as possible. They tend to offer classes that you may join in. If classes are not your speed, then you may want to sign up for a Plant Identification Course. These are offered by universities, community colleges, nurseries, and other plant related societies that are in your area. To maximize the amount of knowledge from these courses, opt for courses that focus on the plants that are native to your area.

A good tip for when you forage is to select plants that have not been exposed in any way to pesticides, the fumes from cars and any object that uses fossil fuels, herbicides and any potential source of poison. Plants can absorb these poisonous chemical compounds which may pass on to you when you eat them. These toxins will not be washed away entirely hence it would be best to simply avoid plants that have been exposed to these types of poisons.

Once you have ascertained that the plant that you intend to forage is not poisonous, the next step would be to subject it to the Universal Edibility Test that will be discussed later on in this book. This test makes sure that you will not experience any ill effects if you decide to eat the plant. Remember the importance of the right part at the right stage of development at the right time for when you forage plants. You can now add the right place to this set of criteria for when you begin to forage in your nearby field.

2.2 WHERE TO FIND YOUR EDIBLES

To find the edible wild plants that you may safely consume, you do not need to head anywhere special, especially if you intend to harvest more common wild plant varieties such as chickweed and dandelions. The beauty of these edible wild plants is that they are able to grow in a variety of areas, such as in your local parks, and anywhere that could allow a plant to thrive. A common link with these areas is that they have been touched by humans before, and because of these, they are able to allow wild plants to thrive. The disadvantage is that, since these plants are wild, they can be anywhere, so if you require several edible species, you will need to devote time to search them out properly, since it is unlikely that these plants would grow in the same areas. Be familiar with the sites that you find the edible wild plants in, they would become a place where you can easily replenish your supply of the plant. You would also need to familiarize yourself with the cycle of development of the plant so you would be able to harvest the plants at the right stage and at the right time. Some plants tend to yield bountiful harvests at certain times so a good practice would be to ensure that you are familiar with their growth cycles and seasonality.

If you are fortunate enough to have a backyard, you could source some of your edible wild plants from your yard. You would have to be aware of any pesticides, herbicides and other chemicals that you may have used in your yard as these would be absorbed by all the plants in your yard. If you happen to live near a park, you would need to ask about the presence of any chemicals and sprays that they use on their plants and any regulations that involve the harvest of wild plants within park premises. Rural parks tend to use lesser amounts of sprays to no sprays at all as they tend to let nature run its course. Urban parks may use larger amounts of sprays and often post signs that warn that an area has been sprayed and indicate what type of spray has been used. If your home is adjacent to any green areas, be warned that if these areas are sprayed with chemicals, nearby plants

may have also absorbed some of the chemicals. To ensure that the plants you forage are chemical free:

» Leave a distance of approximately a hundred feet from the nearest road or path. If you are in a rural area, on a dirt road, a distance of fifteen to twenty feet is enough to ensure that your plants remain toxin free.

» When you are on hilly terrain, it is best to harvest plants that are located uphill from a road as these are located away from the sources of toxins compared to plants that are located downhill from a road. Particulates from car exhaust and sprays travel downwards rather than up.

» You may encounter plants that are located near animal waste, but these are of a lesser concern than plants that are located near sources of heavy metals. It is easier to wash away animal waste rather than the heavy metals that the plants have absorbed.

» If the plant that you intend to harvest is a root crop, exercise caution especially when the area is close to soil contaminants as the root crop could readily absorb these components which would make the plant unsafe to eat.

Once you harvest your edible wild plants, be sure to test out a small amount first before you enjoy your meal. You may be allergic to the plant and in this manner, you would forestall any anaphylactic reactions should you be allergic to the plant.

2.3 SEASONS OF HARVEST

With edible wild plants, you can expect that like their cultivated relatives, they are at their best when you harvest these plants at certain seasons. There are wild plants that are best harvested just after winter and on the first days of springtime. There are also plants whose fruits are at their best once they ripen in the summer time. Some edible wild plants have their most edible parts at their best once winter begins to set in. We repeat once more, the general rule that it is best to learn when to harvest a plant, especially since their parts must be harvested at a specific stage for these to retain their edibleness.

A good idea is to familiarize yourself with the area that you intend to forage in. A good forager would be able to identify plants that grow in a specific area. Once you have identified the area

where the plant that you would like to forage for grows, it would be best to observe the plant as it grows so you will be able to note when they reach a specific stage of development that you may harvest what you need from the plant.

There is no singular best time to identify when a plant is best foraged. However, there are generalizations that can be made that depend on which part of the plant you intend to gather. If the edible plant part you intend to use are the leaves, then these are best gathered when the leaves are young and tender in texture. Greens that are characterized by a bitter and spicy flavor are at their best when harvested at this stage. Older leaves have the tendency to intensify these flavors and this may depend on your preference if you want leaves whose bitter or spicy tastes are more concentrated. When you do harvest leaves, it is best to harvest from plants that have new growths. This often takes place before the plants begin to flower or once plants have begun to re-seed, usually in the fall months. Leaves are best gathered towards the midmorning hours, where the dew on the leaves has evaporated but the sun has not heated the leaves enough to wilt. It is expected that when you harvest plants in the afternoon, that the leaves have undergone wilting due to the heat.

If the edible plant part happens to be a flower, such as chicory, dandelion and elder; these flowers are best harvested when they are about to reach their peak as their flavors are more concentrated at this time. Like leaves, these flowers are best picked in the midmorning before the sun has had the chance to wilt them. Because these are flowers, there are high chances that you may encounter honeybees. Exercise extreme caution if you encounter honeybees, more so if you are allergic to bee stings. Honeybees can be aggressive if they believe that their food source is threatened.

If the edible plant part grows underneath the soil, then these are best gathered in the fall and winter months. These plants include the roots, tubers (such as potatoes) and bulbs, which are gathered once their tops have dried out or were rendered dormant by winter. These roots are best gathered in the winter season until such time that there is new growth by springtime. This is a crucial stage as one new growths begin to emerge from the plant, the structure of the root begins to change into a more fibrous arrangement which renders that part of the plant inedible. Not all roots undergo this structure however, as plants like wild leeks, wild onions and wild garlic retain the same texture when they are harvested once spring sets in, especially when the plant is quite young, and its leaves and other parts are still tender. Be sure to take note on where you have sourced your wild plants so you would ensure that you have a reliable source for your wild plants for future use once you become accustomed to foraging. Should the edible part of the plant be the seeds, such

as Amaranth, be the reason why you harvest, these seeds are usually best gathered in the autumnal months, although this can be altered to be harvested in the late summer. Gather seeds when you have a clear day, best results are yielded when you forage for wild seeds and grains three days or more after the last rainfall in your area. With a pair of sharp scissors, cleanly snip the head of the plant with the seed and store it upside down inside a paper bag. Several seed heads may be stored in the same manner as long as there is enough air to circulate around the seed heads. Once you have harvested the amount that you need, simply shake the paper bag. Matured seeds will fall into the bag. If the seeds are immature, you can leave the seed heads inside the paper bag and store in a warm, dry place. This would allow the seeds to mature, given enough time, the seeds will fall off once they have matured and have been shaken in the bag. Do not allow the bag to be moistened or dampened as this would cause the seed heads to sprout mold. If this happens, spread out the seed heads out in the sun that they may dry and inhibit the growth of mold.

2.4 A "Fruit"ful Harvest

One of the more popular fruits that are gathered by foragers in the wild are the fruits and nuts produced by the edible wild plants in our respective areas. These fruits and nuts tend to stay in season longer than the root crops, leaves and other parts of the edible wild plant. These fruits and nuts are often found in berry patches, fruit trees and nut trees. As with other areas where you forage, always keep an eye on the level of activity in an area. Animals tend to frequent berry patches and trees whose fruits and nuts are ripe. This means that if you notice a larger amount of animal droppings that means it is the right time for you to forage for your berries and nuts from this area. When you begin to harvest your fruits, be sure to choose the fruits that are already ripened to begin with. Unlike our fruits from the grocery, these do not ripen once they have been harvested. A good way to identify if the fruit and nuts are ripened is if they release easily into your hand once you pull. There are instances where you can also find fruits and nuts that are fully ripened on the ground. Be sure to wash them thoroughly before you use them in any recipe. Once you harvest though, it is important that you also respect the cycle of nature. Humans are not the only ones who consume fruits and nuts, as many animals such as birds and squirrels rely on the fruits and nuts as their main source of food to last them throughout the winter. There are animals who may become aggressive if you begin to forage for food that is in their territory. Bears especially, can be quite territorial and will attack if startled. To avoid this, be sure to make your presence known. Bring a companion so you can make enough noise to let any animal know that you are there. If you

are a solitary forager, be sure to sing to yourself or use a bear bell, kept ringing while you forage. Be sure to exercise caution regardless of these measures. Once you have foraged for what you need, be sure to consume these fruits and nuts immediately. They do not last long without any form of preservation and will go bad within three days or so in accordance with your climate.

2.5 THE FORAGERS' KIT

To forage in the woods and fields, it is important that you have a list of tools that would be invaluable to the forager, regardless of the skill level of their expertise. They are quite simplistic in their design and chances are you may have these items in your home.

- » **Backpacks** are an essential tool for the forager due to its storage capacity. When you choose a backpack, search for various compartments that can be used to safely store your tools. You will want enough compartments as well for drinks and a snacks to tide you over as you forage. The main compartment of the bag should be well-padded, so that the plants that you forage are well protected from all the movement that takes place in their transport.

- » **Belts** are useful addition to the forager's kit, and these are dependent on the length of time and the amount of plants you intend to forage. Utility belts are recommended if you intend to keep items such as your scissors and garden shears handy, as well as a few paper bags and other miscellaneous items you feel you would need. Tool belts are handy for the same reason. The type of belt that you would choose is really dependent upon your needs as a forager.

- » **Pocket knives** are at their best when they are short and stout in structure. You will want a pocket knife with a sturdy blade, not one with numerous attachments like a Swiss Army knife, but again, this is dependent on your needs as a forager.

- » **Scissors** are best used for when you need to harvest the smaller, more delicate structures of the plants. Because of their utility in the harvest of the plant parts, they need not be large or expensive, but must be at least sharp.

- » **Garden Shears** are another useful tool. Be sure to select garden shears that you can easily use with one hand, as you will use the other hand to collect the harvested plant

part. The garden shears are optimal for the harvest of grains and plants with woody stems. Proper care of your garden shears includes lubrication and cleaning after every forage. These would allow your garden shears to be useful for several years.

» **Gloves** are useful especially when they are thick enough to withstand the defense mechanisms of plants such as thorns and burrs. A good pair of gloves will provide you with sufficient protection from thorns, burrs and brambles, especially if you intend to cut through the latter to harvest for berries.

» **Trowels** used for foraging are small in size, and are quite sharp. These are best used for roots, tubers and trowels. The small size is a necessity as it would not cause as much disturbance to the soil compared to the use of a larger trowel. Once you are done with your trowel, clean and dry it carefully to extend the length of time that you can use your trowel in.

» **Spray Misters** are useful to keep your foraged plants moist, that they would not dry as you forage for more plants. Use the spray mister once you have placed your harvest into a bag or basket. This way, the mist on the leaves prevents the loss of water from the process of transpiration and gives you wild plants that are crisp and fresh.

» A **Regional Plant Identification Guide** is a handy tool for many foragers to help you identify the plants that are in your native region. This guide, usually small in size, would help you not only identify the edible wild plants that you may need, but also avoid the plants that are poisonous or are just unpalatable.

» **Maps** are there to ensure that you do not get lost and allow you to identify the area where you foraged. If money is not an issue, you can also invest in a GPS for the same purposes. It would be best to carry both items as backups of each other as the GPS can lost its signal the farther you get from civilization, especially if you are concentrated on the foraging.

» **Baskets and paper bags** are ideal containers for the storage of the foraged plants as these allow the plants to breathe with the additional air circulation. Plastic does not afford the plants additional air circulation. Plastic water jugs are ideal for the transport of fruits and nuts, once modified enough that you can hang it from your belt. If you intend to forage for a lot of your food, always have enough containers needed to store your food.

» **Ziploc Bags** are preferred by some foragers due to the light weight and ease by which they can carry and label the plants that they have foraged. This is also ideal as you would be able to readily separate one specie from another.

» **Optional tools for foragers** who favor immediate gratification for their foraged edibles include the use of salad bowls, condiments in packets, and a utensil to consume the foraged food with.

2.6 OUR RESPONSIBILITY TO NATURE

An important responsibility that each forager should consider is the impact that we have upon the Earth. Traditionally, the idea of conservation is commonly associated with the idea of living off the Earth. There is the question though, as to what happens when there are too many of us who decide to do the same act. The concern now is that how can one preserve the edible wild plants if there are too many who wish to forage from nature as well. It is paramount that when you engage in the acts of a forager, you must inculcate within yourself, the responsibilities to care for the earth and maintain stewardship over its resources. Thus, when we harvest, it is necessary to exercise good judgment to ensure that we have enough of the plant for our needs, and leave enough for the plant to survive and replenish itself. It is also up to us to ensure that we are able to harvest in moderation, to ensure that there are enough fruits and nuts for instance, to help populate the area with more of the wild plants, and that the animals themselves have enough food for their needs. There is a distinction that should be made with the foragers, who wish to forage for their personal dietary needs; and the wild crafters, who can potentially overharvest a plant.

There is a basic rule that a forager should keep in mind: **Never take more than what can be easily replaced.** Another key rule should be added for when you harvest from the edible wild plant: **Harvest in a manner that does the least damage to the plant and to the environment around it.** It is essential that when you harvest the edible wild plants, you do so in a manner that is sustainable, and that you enact practices that do not result in the overharvest of the plant. How would you do this then? First off would be to identify if an edible wild plant is endangered or rare. If the plant is classified as either of the two, it would be best to leave these plants and substitute them for another more common edible wild plant. It is also good practice to never take the plant in its entirety unless they are common enough in your area, and are present in such abundance. Plants like these include the dandelion, garlic mustard and chickweed, which are numerous enough in

quantity in most areas that the removal of the entire plant does not adversely impact an entire ecosystem. If you do manage to come across a large patch of plants that can be foraged, do not overharvest them despite their abundance. Foragers who are more accustomed to the plant utilize the two-thirds rule, wherein one harvests only a third of the plant, with the remainder two-thirds of the plant are left behind in the foraging spot. Harvest in a manner that does not damage the plant or its environment, and tread carefully otherwise you may trample newer growths of the plant. To ensure sustainability of the plant, be sure to scatter ripe seeds that you may have to increase the areas where you can harvest the plant in the future, and this way, you are able to reduce your overall environmental impact. This practice is called ethical harvesting, and this is always kept in mind when you forage in the wild for your plants.

2.7 CONCLUSION

The forager has a useful skill that dates back to prehistory as one of the main skills that enabled our ancestors to survive. Though the act remains the same, the steps that are involved in it have changed to accommodate modern tools, and modern problems. Because of the additional knowledge afforded to us by foragers who are experienced in their field, foragers such as yourself are able to gain the necessary knowledge that would enable us to identify the best parts of a plant to eat, how to eat it , when to harvest it, and how to harvest it. This enables us to live off the earth, but this also means that we have a responsibility to care for the earth that we forage from as well. It is a well-executed balance that means that we should care for the earth, just as it provides for us with the food that we can eat.

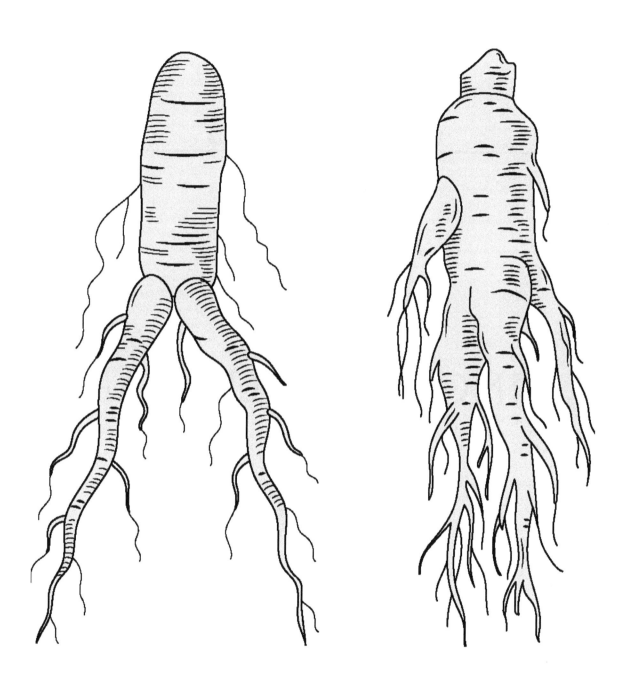

Chapter 3

TAMING THE WILD PLANTS

In this chapter, we begin to understand the lore needed on how to properly use the edible wild plants that we are able to forage. In the previous chapter, we have discussed about our roles as a forager in nature, and how to identify the best times to harvest the edible parts of a plant, and the tools that we need to safely harvest and properly store these foraged plants. This chapter discusses the nutritional benefits that we can obtain from the foraged plants and how to properly store them to maximize their freshness and how to prepare each parts. An important section of this chapter is the Universal Edibility Test that is an essential skill for each forager regardless of their level of expertise. Lastly, we also talk about the poisonous plants that are in the wild, and how we can avoid them.

3.1 NUTRITIONAL VALUE OF WILD PLANTS

We reiterate our discussion on what makes a wild plant edible, or any plant really regardless of their state of cultivation. The simplest definition of edibility is that a plant is safe for human consumption. With the numerous species of plants, it becomes necessary to distinguish those that can be cultivated, those that are naturally wild but still edible, plants that are not edible but are not poisonous, and plants that are poisonous. Chances are you may run into any combination of these four categorizations when you forage for the edible wild plants in the forests and fields.

It is important that you do not let first impressions ruin your idea of what makes a plant edible. The prickly pear cactus is a classic example of the adage "Do not judge a book by its cover". The spines of the cactus may daunt a forager who first comes across it, but once you are able to remove the spines, the pads of the cactus, the flowers and the fruit of the prickly pear cactus are quite edible and are used in a variety of dishes.

Some plants however, require some form of processing. This does not refer to a complicated chemical process that the foraged plant should undergo, but more mundane methods such as cooking, pickling and other culinary methods that make an unpalatable plant part more acceptable to the human palate. Care would have to be taken that you use the appropriate part of the plant, and that it is processed properly to maximize the amount of nutrients that you can get from the plant.

If you are new to the idea of foraged food, you may initially use these wild plants to substitute varieties that you can purchase in town. There is an inherent difference in their flavor and texture, which you may find out once you have tasted the foraged produce, and you may come up with ways that are unique to the plant that would maximize the flavor that each plant contains. It is recommended that at first, you try to cook a small portion of the foraged plant to see if it is suitable for a particular dish, and to see if you have any allergic reactions to it. It takes time to know where a wild plant can be best used, and a lot of experimentation with flavor combinations and the culinary techniques that would bring out the best in the plant and the best of your culinary prowess.

Suffice it to say that because these edible wild plants are not cultivated, the general tendency is that these are more nutrient rich than their cultivated relatives. Remember that cultivated plants are grown in soil that has been farmed. Because the soil has been farmed, the soil has been leached of its nutrients and requires fertilization and enrichment to make it grow some more. As a result, the cultivated varieties of plants are subject to recalls if certain compounds have been used in the fertilizers of these plants, as you may possible ingest the harmful compound that has been used on the soil of these plants or on the plants themselves. Wild plants on the other hand, flourish where the soil is naturally rich, and thus have more concentrated nutrients than its domesticated relatives. The wilder the plant is, the higher the nutritional content. This is also dependent on the quality of soil and the presence of pollutants, but you have covered this area in the previous chapter, and you know which areas to avoid to get the best nutritional value from your foraged foliage.

3.2 The Transport and Storage of Foraged Plants

Once you have foraged for your wild plants, the next step would be to properly store your plants. The initial step would be to keep them away from sunlight, as continued exposure to the heat of the sun causes the leaves of the plants to lose water and wilt. This can be offset by the use of a spray mister in your foragers' kit, but it would be best to simply avoid it and store the plants away from the heat of the sun. The pads in your backpack would be able to help keep the foraged plants from being crushed by your other harvested plants and your tools, but all the same, the use of a basket, or bags, or even a cooler with ice would work well to not only keep your plants away from sunlight, but also avoid any crushed or bruised produce. If you choose to use ice in your cooler, lay a towel to form a protective layer. Direct exposure to cold temperatures would also damage your plants.

Once you have arrived at your home, the initial step that you should do is to brush all the visible dirt from your plants. If you intend to use these plants immediately, you can choose to wash the plants instead. To store them, plastic produce bags may be used, line with a paper towel to absorb any condensation that may be produced. Store these in the crisper section of your refrigerator. Plants stored in this manner must be used within the next day, or two at the most. Before you use them for culinary purposes, wash the plants.

For fruits and vegetables, you may wash them in a solution made from 2 cups water, ¼ cup of baking soda (sodium bicarbonate), and three tablespoons of white vinegar mixed inside a spray bottle. Shake to combine the mix before you spray it on your food and let your produce sit for five minutes before you rinse off the wash.

3.3 Preparations for Edible Wild Plants

Similar to their cultivated cousins, edible wild plants can be prepared in a variety of ways. Some plants are best used in raw dishes such as salads. Wild fruits and berries add a new dimension of flavors when they are mixed into salads, or eaten as is, just as you would consume regular fruit. It is common practice for foragers to consume their foraged produce such as nuts, fruits and berries as they forage for more produce, so if you do this, you are in good company. The leaves of some of these plants contribute a spicy and bitter flavor to more sedate salad greens such as spinach. All you would need to do is combine these leaves with a salad mix of your own, add a few fruits and nuts

to complement the flavors and you have a new salad dish made with foraged greens, all you have to do now is make a vinaigrette, toss it once more and you're done.

If you search around in your home pantry, you may encounter products that have been sourced from edible wild plants that have undergone processing. Some of these items include:

» Maple Syrup. Ordinarily, we would not associate Maple Syrup with edible wild plants, but the fact remains that it is made from the boiled down sap of the Sugar Maple Tree. It is a tradition to tap the sap of the Sugar Maple Tree in North America as it is a celebration of spring. It is also enjoyed by many, and as a sugar substitute it also makes for great business. Maple Syrup is boiled down in a specialized shelter, with a 40:1 ration of sap to syrup that results in the product that we purchase from our groceries.

» Herbal Teas are another product that can be made from wild edible plants, and are perhaps the more popular application as this can be expanded to include medicinal plants. Items such as chamomile and mint tea along with several other types of plants that you may find within this book can be made into popular herbal teas for your personal consumption.

» Honey, by all rights is a foraged food, although granted it was processed by bees. Honey is nectar from the flowers of edible wild plants that has been processed by bees to become the thick sweetener that we obtain from their hives. This does not mean however, that once you see a beehive in the wild, you can forage honey from it. This is best left to the beekeepers and apiarists who specialize in the care of bees and in the harvest of honey.

» Wild Rice is among the grains that can be foraged and is used as a substitute for more commercially prepared versions of rice.

» Pine Nuts are a popular ingredient used in the preparation of pesto. Pine nuts are the commercially processed seeds of specific species of pine cones. Though most pine trees produce pine nuts, only a few species produce pinecones with seeds large enough for consumption by humans. These trees are usually found in the Mediterranean and the warmer parts of Europe as well as in the southwest of the United States.

» Brazil Nuts are a species that are gathered wild from forest trees that produce a quantity of large seeds which have been propagated by an agouti. Brazil nuts are wild crafted, and are found in the forests of Eastern South America.

» Spices such as File powder (used in Creole cuisine), Szechuan peppercorns (which are not related to the pepper plant but from the prickly ash tree), Bayberry Leaves (used in place of Bay leaves), Spicebush Berries (a substitute for allspice), and Peppergrass Seeds (which make a great substitute for wild mustard) are all foraged from the wild.

» Black Walnuts are a delicacy often integrated in numerous desserts and pastries in Europe and North America and are related to the English walnut. This is commonly found throughout Eastern North America.

» Carrageenan is an emulsifier made from seaweed, and is commonly used to thicken ice creams and other foods that require thickening. It is also used to thicken other household products that are not food.

These are just samples of wild foraged foods that have undergone several processes before they could be used as part of our diet. There are several more preparations that could be undertaken to prepare and store the edible wild plants for human consumption. This next section focuses on the preservation of the produce.

3.4 FOOD PRESERVATION OF EDIBLE WILD PLANTS

Food preservation is a necessary skill for the forager in the event that you were able to harvest a surplus amount of edible wild plants. As a forager, and as a cook, one of the signs of a well-run kitchen is a kitchen that is self-sufficient in its supplies and is thrifty enough to make proper use of the bounty of foraged products. Early hunter-gatherer societies were able to survive the scarcities of winter with the proper preservation of the food that they had gathered over the spring and summer months. In this contemporary age, you, as a forager, have more tools at your disposal. There are four principal methods by which you can preserve the food that you were able to forage: Canning, Freezing, Drying and Cold Storage or the use of a Root Cellar. There are other methods such as Fermentation and Salting. What is important is that, if properly utilized, you are able to prevent and retard the growth of bacteria and mold that would spoil the food that you have harvested.

This section will serve as a guide on which food products are best used under specific preservation techniques. Not all techniques will work for every edible wild plant so it is important to know which technique works best for specific types of plant products. This way you are able to make the most out of your harvest. The techniques you choose would also depend on your taste, the equipment that you have available to preserve the food, and the amount of food that you have in excess that you want to preserve for later use.

Freezing is one of the easiest preservation techniques available to the forager and the cook. It does require a freezer, which many of us own in some form. Apart from the freezer, you will want containers that handle the freezer well. Some plastic containers may be quite flimsy that they shatter when they are subjected to prolonged cold temperatures. When you freeze foods, you require lesser amounts of preparation compared to other methods, and the food is as close to its natural state compared to canned and dried versions. It is however, energy intensive, as your food supply would have to be in a frozen state- unless you live somewhere that is naturally cold. You will also want to be careful with the amount of freezer space you consume, as some food may become bad because of freezer burn. Freezers are best suited for meats, fruit juices and berries and fruits in their raw state.

» To freeze leaves and stems of foraged food,

   o Blanch first. When you blanch the leaves and stems, this stops the chemical activity of the enzymes that cause the plant to degrade faster and preserves the flavor and texture of the plant. It also cleans the plant and makes the color brighter. Lastly, when you blanch the leaves and stems, it makes them more pliable and easier to store in containers in the freezer.

   o Once you blanch the leaves and stems, cool them immediately in an ice water bath to shock them and stop the cooking process. Drain the leaves and stems completely of water before you pack them into the containers to freeze. Be sure that they are free of water otherwise the residual water may form ice, which would affect the taste of the frozen produce.

» To freeze mushrooms, fruits and nuts

   o Mushrooms are best frozen once they have been cooked. They are usually sautéed in some fat (butter or oil), and are frozen together with the liquid produced by them.

o Fruits and berries on the other hand, are frozen individually, rather than frozen to-gether. If you have harvested a plethora of berries, be sure to spread them out on a tray covered with a layer of wax paper, and place the tray into the freezer. Once they have frozen, simply slide the berries into a container so that they can be stored to-gether. The berries are able to maintain their structure in this way, and will be free of ice crystals.

o Nuts can be frozen shelled or unshelled. Freeze nuts if you do not intend to use them within a week after you have harvested them. They contain a high fat content and can spoil if left in room temperature. There are species of nuts that need to be cured or dried before they are shelled. They can be kept frozen for up to a year.

Drying is another food preservation technique that is best suited for leaves, fruits and roots. This technique allows you to preserve the flavor of the item that is dried. When dried at low temperatures, this allows you to preserve fruits and mushrooms for years. They can be rehydrated and be used as fresh produce. Aside from this, drying is a technique that is used for the preservation of flour, sugar, grains and other food items as this removes the moisture that allows bacteria to grow onto the food.

Once the food has been properly prepared, it can keep without the need for additional equipment compared to freezing. Because the water content of the food causes it to reduce in size, the food takes up lesser storage space. There are several ways that you can preserve food by drying. They may be dried out in the heat of the sun; away from sunlight in a warm place; in a food dehydrator, an oven placed on low heat, or on top of a woodstove. The food may be dried on cloths, screens and boards, but trays seem to yield the best results for when you dry food.

» To dry seeds, grains and nuts, they can be exposed to the sun, laid out on a tarpaulin. They may also be dried at room temperature in a shallow container. Of the foraged produce, these are the easiest to dry as they naturally have a low moisture content.

» Leaves of edible wild plants however, should be dried away from sunlight as the light can bleach the color out of these leaves and leach out the nutrients from the plant itself. You do not need to dehydrate them out in the sun, as water would easily evaporate from the leaves due to the larger surface area. Spread leaves on cloths or any clean surface. You may also tie them up in a bundle, and hang them upside down in a place out of the way.

Once dried, store in an airtight container. This technique is not suited for the leaves of succulent plants as this can cause the plant tissues to become more compacted and less palatable.

» Vegetable shoots are not suited for preservation in this manner as they are quite thick and succulent. Bracken Fern Fiddleheads however may be dried, provided that they have been blanched for a minute before dried out in the sun. Once subjected to a higher temperature, they take on the consistency of dried pasta after six hours of exposure to heat.

» Root crops and tubers may also be dried, once they have been diced or sliced. They can be quite hard once they are dried, but are easily rehydrated once needed for a recipe. Tap roots such as parsnips may be grated or cut finely, or blanched before they are dried.

» Fruits may be quite finicky in their processes compared to that of seeds, nuts and grains, but they are well worth the effort invested in the dehydration process. Smaller fruits and berries may be dried whole with the use of a food dehydrator – a specialized equipment. This equipment is necessary since if fruits these small are subjected to the regular methods, they tend to spoil or lose most of their flavor. The use of the Electric Food Dehydrator consumes a lot of energy that is not proportional to their size and may not be practical for those foragers who tend to dry only a smaller quantity of fruit.

» If you do not wish to invest in a food dehydrator, and frequently dry berries for storage, here is what you can do. Berries may be crushed first, as this allows them to dry faster and prevent their spoilage. You can safely dehydrate them under the heat of the sun without any risk to the quality of their flavor.

» Another method to preserve fruits is through the creation of fruit leather. Fruit leather may be consumed as a snack, or rehydrated for use in stocks, sauces and marinades. Fruits ideal for dehydration into fruit leather include small berries, crab apples, prickly pears and pineapple guava. To dehydrate fruit into fruit leather, the fruit must be first cooked. Spread an even layer of the fruit at the bottom of a large pan and cover with enough water. Be sure to do this over a medium heat until the fruit is softened enough that you can mash it, and puree with the help of a blender. For a smoother product, you may use a food mill to puree the mixture further. Taste the fruit to sweeten, some fruits

are naturally tart and will require additional sweeteners such as honey. If additional sweeteners are needed, return to the pan and sweeten to taste. Allow the fruit to cook over a medium heat until the fruit is spreadable, similar to the consistency of jam, but not runny.

- o If you have a dehydrator, spread this into a smooth, even layer on a fruit-leather sheet lined tray, to a 1/8 inch thickness. This will take 8-12 hours in the dehydrator to fully dry into fruit leather.
- o If you have an oven, line a cookie sheet with a sheet of parchment paper and pour the puree into a 1/8 inch thick layer. Dry at 125-150°F overnight until it resembles pliable leather.
- o For both methods, remove from the tray and cut into strips. Store the fruit leather in an airtight container in the refrigerator.

Canning is a method used by foragers to store sterile food in containers that have been sterilized. These sterilized containers are structured to ensure that they prevent the growth of bacteria, mold and other microorganisms that can cause food to spoil. There are three methods used by foragers: Pressure Canning, Water-Bath Canning and Sterile-Product Canning. Each method is suitable for specific types of wild edible produce and cannot be substituted for another method. From the perspective of one who goes to the grocery, you can see that there are a plethora of foods that are preserved with the use of canning. We do not see much of canned plants however, save that of corn, asparagus, peas, beans and mushrooms. We do not see canned wild plants however, and this is what the book discusses.

Edible wild plants that can be canned include the likes of fiddlehead ferns – bracken and ostrich type, asparagus, milkweed shoots and the young pods, fruit spreads, wild leek bulbs and juices. Once the vegetables have been processed further into cooked versions such as soups, they lend themselves well to the canning process. You would be even able to stockpile portions of homemade canned soup, rather than purchase the factory made ones, or make an entire portion from scratch should you crave soup. Once a food has been canned, there is nothing else that is needed to keep it preserved, unlike the use of a freezer.

There is a danger with canning as a procedure, and many authors have classified it as a high-risk procedure. Provided you take certain safety precautions, you are able to overcome these minimal

risks. Besides, high risk means high reward, with a ready pantry of canned items as your reward. Modern devices and kitchenware have made canning a safer process than it was before. What you should be aware of with the canning process is that there is the risk of food poisoning, especially with *Clostridium botulinum,* a bacteria that appears in improperly canned food and is very deadly if ingested as it is the cause of botulism. Do not let this turn you off from home canned produce however, as you can also experience food poisoning from store bought items, so the risk is basically evened out at this point. A higher risk in the canning process is the potential to scald yourself with the hot water needed, but provided you utilize proper safety measures, you can avert these risks.

To can, you will need a canner, canning jars with two-piece lids, tongs to handle the hot canning jars, and a clean, sterile cloth to wipe up the rims of the jars. Let's discuss canners first:

» Pressure canning uses canners that are purposefully built to accommodate intense amounts of pressure. Preferred brands for foragers include Presto and Mirro, though that would depend on what is readily available in your area.

» Water-bath canning is more versatile as you can use any deep pot with a lid. You just need to make sure that there is a barrier between the canning jars and the bottom of the pot.

» Sterile-product canning does not require the use of a canner.

Canning jars come in several sizes: Half-pint, pint and quarts. Use the half-pint sized canning jars for portions that you do not consume large quantities of at once. This size is best for produce that does not keep well once it has been opened. Quarts are ideal for canned foods that are consumed in large quantities and are best suited for foragers with large families. Single foragers usually opt for the pints and half-pints except for when they store juices from fruits. You may find old canning jars from garage sales but these tend to be more fragile than newly purchased canning jars.

Jar lids come in two sizes: Standard and wide-mouth. Wide-mouth jars do take up more space than the average jar and the lids may be more costly. They are easier to clean than your usual jar and you can easily remove food from it as well. It is not recommended that you use French lids that clamp directly onto the jar, nor is there a need to seal jelly jars with a paraffin layer. All that is needed to develop a seal with your canning jars are a lid and a screw band. You may reuse the screw bands, but you cannot reuse a lid.

» Pressure Canning is recommended for edible wild plants with a low-acid content. These include asparagus, beans, corn, greens, soup, and non-acidic fruits and vegetables. You may also use this method to can meat and dairy products. The pressure in this type of method is needed to kill the spores of the *Clostridium botulinum* bacteria. This type of bacteria is the cause of botulism, and can withstand the boiling point of water, which means that you need to intensify the pressure exerted, to increase the water temperature so that the bacterial spores can be killed.

  o This type of bacteria thrives in a dark, moist, anaerobic environment –such as the inside of a can. They are also found in soil. When they metabolize their food, they exude a toxin called botulin which can be very deadly if ingested. Cases of botulism commonly occur in establishments that deal with food. For the forager who cans at home, botulism may occur in low-acid fruits and vegetables that are canned.

  o To pressure can: purchase a new canner; read the instruction booklet on how to safely use the canner, and keep the booklet for when you need to check on a particular step or method. This booklet is key as many manufacturers publish updated instructions on how to properly can products, so as much as possible, follow the instructions of the manufacturer.

  o To begin the canning process, pack the food that you intend to be canned into the canning jars. There is a question on the need to sterilize canning jars, but this is entirely up to your preference. You can sterilize the canning jars if you wish to, but there is no need to do so as they will be sterilized once they are subjected to the pressure in the canner. The food stored may be pre-cooked, or packed in the jar raw. Take note that the latter option will require longer canning hours. Some edible wild plants such as leaves should never be packed into the canning jar in their raw state. Do not place a hot item into a cold jar or you will break the jar. Use the canning jars at room temperature, but if the jars are older, soak in hot water for a few minutes before you use them in canning.

  o When you pack cooked food items, add some of the cooking water into the canning jars. When you pack the raw food items, pour the boiling water into the jar after you pack the food in. Press along the sides and stir the contents of the jar with a wooden spoon or a spatula to remove any air bubbles. Add more hot water to fill in the spac-

es. For both types of packing, the liquid should cover the food entirely and have a one-inch space before the jar lid.

o The jar rims should not have any bits of food, as any trapped food bits may break the sterile seal created by the pressure canning, or prevent the creation of the seal in the first place. The new lids should be placed on the canning jars and attached firmly. The canning jars are now ready for the canner.

o As you prepare the jars, you should have water heating up in the pressure canner, which should begin to boil the moment you are done packing the canned food. The amount of water you need for the canner depends on the size, you have to check with the instructions provided by the manufacturer. The canner that you use should have a metal shelf that prevents the bottom of the canning jars from reaching the bottom of the canner.

o Screw the lid of the canner on properly and allow it to boil until steam begins to steadily come out of the valve. Allow to steam for 7-10 minutes before you attach the pressure cap. Ideally, the pressure in the canner should reach 10-11 pounds (adjust if you live in a higher altitude area). Lower the heat and count down from the processing time that is stated on the manual of your canner. Adjust the heat to maintain the pressure or above the desired amount of pressure. Do NOT allow the pressure to build up and do NOT leave the canner unattended.

o Pressure canning wild plants may have different times compared to what is stated in the canner's manual. You will need to estimate the time through a comparison of vegetables that are of a similar composition. Process longer if you are unsure.

o Once the food has been processed, switch off the heat. Let the canner release the pressure naturally. Do NOT remove the pressure cap, the sudden change in pressure can cause the jars to expel the packed food and ruin the seal that you made to keep it sterile. Do NOT remove the canner lid until the pressure has completely dissipated – you will know this the moment you remove the pressure cap and there is no more steam or hot air comes out. CAUTION: This step may cause you to be scalded if you do not follow these steps. Once the pressure has been released, open the canner and use tongs to carefully remove the jars.

o Once the jars have been removed from the canner for some time, you will expect to

hear a pop. This means the lids have been sucked downwards due to the decreased pressure in the jars. You will know this has happened if you press the center of the jar lids and they do not move. If the lids have not properly sealed, the centers would be still produce a sound each time you press, If this happens, refrigerate the food and use the contents as soon as possible while you figure out why the jar never sealed in the first place.

o   Once the jars have sealed, remove the screw bands. The suction pressure is enough to keep the seal on the jars. Use the screw bands the next time you can, and clean to prevent the formation of rust. Store the sealed jars in a cool, dry place away from the sunlight, which can cause a chemical reaction with your canned food. Do not let your jars freeze. Label the jars with the type of food and date that they were canned. Follow the FIFO Method (First In, First Out). If the food has an odor once you open it, discard. You may choose to boil the jar first before you consume.

»   Water-Bath Canning is simpler than the principles in pressure canning. This method is recommended for foods with a high-acid content such as fruits, fruit spreads, juices and some vegetables. The high acid content prevents the growth of the *C. botulinum* bacteria, and dispenses with the need for any form of pressure. This type of canning procedure is not suited for fruits with a low acidic content such as figs, dates, olives, and several species of peaches and tomatoes. It is advised that you do not interchange this method with the pressure canning procedure as pressure canning will destroy the flavor of items that are suited for the water bath canning procedure.

o   To do water bath canning, the jars that contain the cooked product are placed in a canning kettle with boiling water that covers the lids by one inch. The products to be canned have to be cooked, water bath canning is NOT advised for raw food. The water is allowed to boil for some time until the jars have been sterilized. The time is dependent on the type of the jar, its size and the texture of the food item that is canned. Liquid is able to move around in the jar as it is canned which allows the heat from the canning kettle to be distributed throughout the contents of the jar. Thicker consistencies of products are unable to move as freely and would take some time to thoroughly heat up and be sterilized.

» Sterile Product Canning is where you heat food until it boils, and while still hot, pack the cooked food into the sterile jars. While still hot, screw the two-piece jar lids onto the packed jars and turn upside-down and leave for a few minutes. The heat from the cooked food will sterilize the jar some more from the inside and the lids. This method is commonly used for thicker and sweeter products such as jams, jellies and syrups. They do not need to be boiled as intensely as the water bath method and the pressure canned method as the high sugar environment prevents the growth of bacteria in the food. These types of food items do not need treatment with the water –bath canning method as the large amounts of sugar that are naturally dissolved with the food are able to increase the temperature within the packed food. As you transfer the cooked jam or jelly into the jar, the temperature would still be hotter than the normal sterilization temperature which ensures that no form of bacteria will be able to grow on your preserved food. If you do use a half-pint sized jar however, you should soak these in hot water or boiling water before you pack food into them as the thickness of the glass could cause the food to cool down faster before its temperatures could even sterilize the jar. This process does NOT accommodate jars that are smaller than a half-pint.

The last type of preservation method that is used by foragers to preserve their foraged produce is the use of the cold storage method. This method is alternatively called the root cellar method and should not be confused with the use of freezing as a preservation method. This carries its own distinct purposes and can only be used with specific parts of food. The purpose of cold storage is to keep the plant alive, but dormant. Plants are still living organisms and require certain methods by which it can survive. If left without water, they dehydrate. If they are exposed to low temperatures, the frost can kill them. Our previous preservation methods involve the death of a plant, morbid as it sounds. We chop them up, cook them, then can, freeze or dry them. In cold storage however, the difference is that the plant is still alive, and because it is still alive, the plant cannot spoil.

Cold storages may be done with the aid of a refrigerator, but this can be costly, especially if you have high energy costs, and if your fridge is filled with other produce that you have preserved. There is a more economically viable alternative with the use of the root cellar, suitable if you have foraged large amounts of root crops and need somewhere to store them safely. A root cellar, from the latter part, means that this area is located underground. It becomes economical as due to its location beneath the Earth, the cellar uses the naturally insulation to maintain a steady temperature with

cool temperatures and enough moisture to allow you to store your fruits and vegetables. You may find root cellars in the basement of your home, this is the more modern application. Traditional root cellars are often kept separate from the home, constructed underground or into the side of a hill or a large enough amount of soil.

This does not mean however, that you should now take up a shovel and begin to dig a root cellar around your home. For one you may have zoning laws to contend with, not to mention a lot of permits. If you do not have a basement or a handy hill that you can use for your root cellar, you can apply the same idea on a smaller scale. A bucket would be sufficient if you only foraged a small amount of root vegetables. Cover the foraged root crops with enough leaves until the weather becomes cold enough that you can bring it into your home and store it in the coldest parts of your home. While this is not as ideal as the root cellar, you will still be able to preserve your root crops for a longer period of time.

Cold storage is ideal as it allows you to safely store plants in their most natural state, which allows you to enjoy their flavors even after they are no longer seasonal. It is also a low-cost, low-energy way to preserve food, compared to canning, freezing and drying. It has a disadvantage in that only certain parts of the plants may be preserved in this manner.

» Only parts of the food that are able to produce and grow on their own may be preserved in cold storage – such as the taproots and tubers. This means that leafy plants cannot be preserved through the use of the cold storage method, except if you intend to preserve the whole plant. You can however, store some fruit in this manner, such as cranberries and apples. When you store fruit with the use of the cold storage method, the fruit must be undamaged. Gather the fruit that you intend to store and arrange in a box or crate and layer with wood shavings, old (yet dry) newspapers, or virtually any object that would stop the flow of air in between the fruit. This insulated layer ensures that there is little moisture loss from the fruit that is stored.

» Cold storage is best suited for root crops that can be foraged for in large quantities. These include the likes of the wild carrot, Jerusalem artichoke (sunchoke), parsnips, evening primrose, hopniss, burdock root, wapato and thistle roots. To store these root crops, arrange loosely in a bin or bucket and carefully cover with items that inhibit the loss of moisture. You may cover these with sphagnum moss, leaves, moist sand, sawdust or even newspapers. The vegetables are able to withstand a light amount of frost as they

are naturally subjected to this in their regular environment. It is important that you take the precautions needed to protect them from the hard freeze that can cause your vegetable store to spoil.

» To harvest the root crops for storage, carefully dig around the area of the plant and ensure that the root that you harvest has not been bruised, cut or nicked by your tools. If there is some form of damage, you should use them as soon as possible. The root crops should not touch or have minimal contact, and the material in which they are packed in must be changed when they have dried out. The roots best keep when they are maintained in a temperature that keeps them frozen, without any changes.

3.5 THE UNIVERSAL EDIBILITY TEST

As a forager, you are expected to be well versed with the plant life that you have foraged in your locale. It is expected that you have the necessary knowledge to tell apart the plants that are suitable for consumption and those that should be avoided at all costs. There are plant species however, that are similar to edible plants and are not edible at all. The problem is, no matter how much knowledge we have, there may come a time that in all due confidence, we forage for a plant thought to be edible and later find out that the plant was a similar looking, yet toxic variety. To circumvent this botanical conundrum, we now talk about the Universal Edibility Test.

The Universal Edibility Test allows you to determine if a plant is edible; and further assess that if the plant is edible, that you do not suffer from an allergic reaction to it should you consume it. The test itself takes some time to utilize when you forage, but it is better to be safe than sorry. It is expected that in the course of experimentation that you would be subjected to some adverse reactions from certain plants, as you would need to know if you are allergic to them. If you are allergic, it would be best to have your medication with you, or have a companion with you who can administer first aid should the adverse effect result in anaphylactic shock.

To perform the test, you should separate the parts of the plant into their basic structures. Similar to science class, you will want to ensure that the leaves, flowers, roots, petals, sepals, buds, stems and other parts of the plant have been identified and separated. Remember, it was discussed earlier that some parts of the plant may be edible while the rest of the plant is not. This way, it would be

easier to take note of which part of the plant you are actually allergic to, or have adverse reactions to.

TIP: Before you embark on your experiment with the Universal Edibility Test, it would be more prudent to have several species of the same plants with you as you perform the steps for the test. This may be exhaustive, but this works in two ways. Best case, the plant is edible and you have an immediate supply of the edible wild plant. Worst case, you develop and adverse reaction and head towards the emergency department, the extra plants will help the physicians identify the compound your body has reacted to and you can be treated of your adverse reactions faster.

» Contact is the first step in the test to determine edibility of a plant. To perform this you first:

  o Press a bit of the plant part and rub a bit of the juice that it exudes onto different areas of your skin. **Take note of which part is applied on where on your skin. This will help you when you need treatment for an adverse reaction**. Ideally, this juice should be placed on the more sensitive parts of your skin such as the insides of your wrists and the inner skin on your elbows. Once applied, leave the juice on these areas for at least fifteen minutes except if you develop an adverse reaction to the juice. Adverse reactions can take the form of itchiness, urticarial (hives) and burning. If the latter three occur, wash your skin of the juice with soap and water and stop the test.

  o If there is no immediate reaction from the juice of the plant on your skin, it would be best to wait eight hours before you check for any other reaction such as itchiness, burning or urticaria. If you experience these symptoms, wash the affected area with soap and water and stop the test.

  o If you do not have any reaction to the plant juices, move on to the next step.

  o If you are sensitive to specific parts of the plant, cease the test with those parts and move on to the other parts of the plant.

  o The lip test may be used to determine further sensitivity to the plant. Hold a part of the plant to your lips one at a time, and take note of which part was held to it. Adverse reactions include burning and tingling sensations and you should stop the test if this happens and cleanse your lips with soap and water to wash off any allergens. Resume this test **ONLY** if your lips have returned to their normal state.

» Tasting and Chewing are the next steps to determine the edibility of a plant. You may proceed to this step of the Universal Edibility Test if and only if you have not experienced any adverse reactions from the Lip Test and the Contact Test in the previous step.

- o The taste portion of the test is performed when you place a piece of the plant part on your tongue and leave it for fifteen minutes. Similar to the contact part of the test, adverse reactions to the plant are indicated by a burning or itching sensation. If this occurs, spit it out and wash your mouth with water. Continue with the test **ONLY** if your mouth feels and looks normal. (**NOTE: You will want somebody to be with you at this point to ensure that you are able to have access to first aid and immediate medical care**)

- o The chewing portion of the test will take place **ONLY** after you have reassured that you will not have an adverse reaction from the taste test in the previous step. If no reactions have been detected from the plant in the previous step, chew it but **DO NOT** swallow. Keep the chewed up plant in your mouth for fifteen minutes. If you feel a burning or itching sensation, spit out the plant and rinse your mouth with water.

» The Swallow Test is the last part of the Edibility Test and will take place only after a negative Chew Test result. If a negative chew test is recorded, you may swallow the plant. This step is the longest in the test as you would have to forego any other form of food or drink, aside from water, when you are in this portion of the test. This is because if you ingest other food or drink while you undertake this portion of the test, and develop an adverse reaction, it would be difficult to determine if you were allergic to either the plant you swallowed, the other food or drink you ingested, or if you were allergic to both. Be sure that when you perform this part of the test, you have not eaten anything beforehand to avoid the same confusion.

- o Once you have swallowed the plant part, wait for eight hours. Keep yourself hydrated with water, but do not ingest any other food or drink. Adverse reactions will now take the form of nausea, and if you feel this, induce the vomit reflex and seek medical treatment. If you are fine after eight hours since you swallowed the plant, proceed to the next step.

- Eat only the plant part for this part of the test. Do not add any other item such as salt, pepper, vinaigrettes, or condiments. The amount of the plant that you consume should only be ¼ cup. Wait for eight more hours and be sure to keep hydrated with water. If you begin to feel nausea, induce vomiting and seek medical attention.

» The test will take time to administer, and it is permissible to conduct the test on separate days. If you choose to do this step, be sure that you do not take any other food or drink eight hours before you plan to perform the tests to avoid any potential interactions and confusion with the food you have eaten previously.

» If the plant needs to be processed before you can test it, especially for plants that require cooking to be edible, or to reduce the bitterness of their taste, you may boil or bake the plant. Follow the same steps in the test as you perform the test on the plant. The test will take a lot of time, but it is better to be safe than to be poisoned by a plant.

3.6 The Identification of Poisonous Plants and how to Avoid Them

In the previous section, one of the steps required to perform the Edibility Test is to have several of the same species of plants when you perform the test. There are instances where plants present with similar characteristics, but are actually quite poisonous if you are unable to identify them correctly. Some poisonous plants are readily identifiable as they tend to have irritants that immediately affect you once you come into contact with them. Some poisonous plants are characterized by glossy leaves and bright red fruits but others may present similarly to other more edible species hence the need for extra care, and the use of this section to guide you through. There are three guidelines that would help you avoid poisonous plants:

1. Be familiar with the poisonous plants that thrive in the areas that you usually forage in. Learn about what they look like and take note if they bear any similarity to edible wild plants that you forage for in the area.

2. Before you perform the Universal Edibility Test, identify all the plants in the area. When you are in doubt, throw it out.

3. If there are poisonous plants that grow near a patch of plants that you know are edible, **DO NOT** harvest the edible wild plants as they may have been contaminated with the slightest amount of poison from these plants. The smallest amount of toxins ingested is enough to exert a deadly effect on your body.

Characteristics of plants that are poisonous in some state include these features:

» If the plant has **Bristly Hairs**, this means that the plant is likely to be a skin irritant. Not all plants that have bristly hairs are poisonous though, as this is also shared by some edible wild plants.

» If the plant has **Bulbs, Beans, or Seeds located inside Pods**, they should be generally avoided unless you are certain that these are of the edible variety.

» Plants whose leaves resemble that of dill, parsley or carrots are most likely toxic.

» Plants that emit **a scent reminiscent of almonds** from its leaves or wood should be avoided as they contain cyanide. Cyanide is found in many plants and is characterized by an aroma that smells like almonds.

» Plants that have Bitter Smells, a scent similar to Soap, or taste soapy are generally quite toxic.

» Plants that exude a sap similar to milk, or if the sap changes color once exposed to air may be toxic. Test carefully.

» Plants that have grain heads with **black, pink or purple spurs** should be avoided at all times.

Common Poisonous Plants include the Anthurium, Chrysanthemum, Ficus, Foxglove, Hydrangea, Lily of the Valley, the Narcissus, Oleanders, Rhododendrons and Wisteria.

3.7 CONCLUSION

Throughout this section, we have discussed the benefits that you can obtain when you consume wild plants and how you can safely store them for longer periods especially for the winter months. An important section for this chapter is the identification of edible plants with the Universal Edibility Test and the identification of poisonous plants. It is necessary to exercise caution when

you forage for plants in the wild as the compounds in some plants may induce adverse reactions in the body that require immediate medical assistance, hence the numerous tests and precautions that you must undertake before you begin to forage for a plant. Now that we have you kitted out to forage, and taught you the basics on how to preserve your foraged produce, the next chapter delves into the types of edible wild plants that you can forage for in your fields and forests.

pine nut

almond

walnut

hazelnut

coconut

cashew

peanut

sunflower seed

pistachio

cola nut

pumpkin seed

pecan nut

Chapter 4

A COMPENDIUM OF EDIBLE WILD PLANTS

For the purposes of organization, the plants listed here will have their Common Names; Description; Distinguishing Characteristics; Location; Seasonality; How to Harvest the Plant; Flavor Profiles; Edible Parts; Serving Suggestions and Other Uses; and Precautions.

4.1 AMARANTH (AMARANTHUS SPP.)

Common Name: The Amaranth is also known as Pigweed, Callaloo and Kallaloo.

Description: The stems of the Amaranth are erect and range from a vibrant green to a deep red in color. The lower portion of the stem tends to be thick and smooth, interspersed with spines. The upper portion of the stem as a contrast, is very rough and is riddled with sharp hairs – its defense mechanism. The leaves of the Amaranth are arranged alternately on its stem. They are oval in shape, broad at their base and tapers to a tip; and are colored from a dull green to a lustrous reddish-green. The Amaranth has flowers that are small and green, clustered around the top of the plant with smaller clusters along the axes of the leaves. These flowers later produce tiny, but very nutritious seeds.

Distinguishing Features: The plant, if left alone, may grow up to six feet in abandoned places; but it may reach a height of two to three feet once matured.

Location: The Amaranth grows all over North America, in areas where there is soil disturbance. Ideally, it is found in gardens, abandoned fields and livestock pastures.

Seasonality: Amaranth usually presents in the springtime and are able to survive until the last days of winter. The plant is able to propagate itself and because of this, younger plants may be found in a lot of areas, throughout all the seasons. The matured Amaranth, with its seeds, are found from the later parts of summer to fall.

Harvest: To harvest the Amaranth, simply snip it with a pair of garden shears. Follow the steps to harvest the seed heads.

Flavor Profile: The leaves of the Amaranth have a flavor reminiscent to that of Spinach. The seeds have a milder taste.

Edible Parts: You may only consume the leaves and seeds of the Amaranth.

Serving Suggestions and Other Culinary Applications: The Amaranth leaves are ideal for use in salads or may be prepared in recipes that use similar types of greens. The seeds may be turned into sprouts, and tossed with any type of salad. They may also be eaten on their own, they may be lightly toasted or they can be popped in the same manner as popcorn. In the latter application, they may also be mixed in with other grains and dried fruits for your own granola or trail mix. Toasted, they may be ground into a gluten-free flour for use in various applications.

Precautions: The plant may overrun other plants if cultivated so care would have to be taken to control it. Wear gloves as a precaution as the spiny hairs on its stems can become thorns if harvested late into the season.

4.2 ARROWROOT (SAGITTARIA LATIFOLIA)

Common Name: Arrowroot, Indian Potato, Duck Potato, Wapato, Broadleaf Arrowhead, Tsee Goo.

Description: The Arrowroot is an aquatic plant with tapered leaves shaped like arrowheads. The small white flowers are arrayed on stalks, where the flowers are above the leaves. The root of the plant resembles a bulb and

is pale in color. The root varies in size, from a few inches in diameter, to the approximate size of a chicken egg.

Distinguishing Features: The veins of the arrowroot leaves are arranged parallel to each other. The blossoms of the plant have three petals.

Location: You may find the arrowroot anywhere in North America, where it thrives along ponds and the lakeshores. They are also found along the banks of rivers with a slow current, especially where the river meanders.

Seasonality: They are best harvested in the late summer to late fall.

Harvest: You will expect to be messy when you harvest arrowroot given its proclivity towards the water, where it grows beneath the soil, underneath a layer of water. A large bucket is necessary for you to be able to wash the harvested arrowroot. To harvest it, you may use a large stick or a pitchfork to carefully detach the arrowroot from the plant. They float to the surface readily so you can just pick it up and wash it.

Flavor Profile: The arrowroot is mildly flavored, similar to a chestnut or a potato.

Edible Parts: The arrowroot has only one edible part, the fleshy corm or tuber that you harvest.

Serving Suggestions and Other Culinary Applications: You may eat the arrowroot in its raw state, but it may also be prepared as you would a potato: fried, boiled or roasted. The arrowroot may be sliced thinly and dried before it is ground into a gluten-free flour. This flour is often used as a thickener and may be used as a substitute for corn starch in cooking. Arrowroot flour has twice the thickening power of wheat flour and is tasteless in its ground state so it does not impart any additional flavor into the food.

Precautions: A similar specie to this is the Arrow Arum which often grows alongside the plant. The leaves of this specie however, have a single midrib and side veins, and has a long, taproot similar to a parsnip or carrot. This specie is inedible.

4.3 Bay Laurel (Laurus nobilis)

Common Name: Laurel, Bay Laurel, Sweet Bay, Bay Tree

Description: The laurel is an evergreen, which can take the form of a bushy shrub or a tree. It does reach a maximum height of fifty nine feet so you would need to consider that as well. The laurel leaves are pointed, long and have a glossy finish to its dark green foliage that gives it a leathery sensation when touched. The blooms of the laurel are yellow-green in color and when matured, produce small black berry-like structures called drupes that are at least a centimeter in diameter.

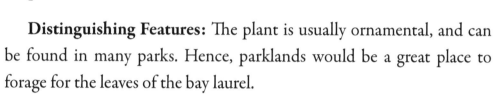

Distinguishing Features: The plant is usually ornamental, and can be found in many parks. Hence, parklands would be a great place to forage for the leaves of the bay laurel.

Location: The tree itself originates from the Mediterranean region where it thrives in the warmth, but is sensitive to the cold. The tree prefers areas that rarely encounter the formation of frost. It enjoys the sun and soil that is moist, but well-drained. It can also thrive however, in shady areas and poor soils. As an indoor plant, it can be regularly pruned and stored in a smaller container.

Seasonality: The plant, as an evergreen, is available year round. If you intend to propagate the plant for your personal use, it is best to take a cutting on the transition period between summer and fall.

Harvest: Simply pick the leaves from the tree.

Flavor Profile: The leaves of the laurel can be both sweet and savory, but use sparingly as too much of the leaf can make any dish quite bitter.

Edible Parts: The leaves, but do not consume the leaves. They are used in cuisine for flavor.

Serving Suggestions and Other Culinary Applications: The leaves are often used as an herb or as a spice, alone or with other herbs in a bouquet garni. Whole leaves may be added to stews or soups or stuffed inside poultry or beneath the skin of the bird. The leaves may be dried for other

purposes. Medicinally, the leaves in the form of essential oils are able to ease altitude sickness and prevent tooth decay.

Precautions: It can irritate the skin so be careful. Do not swallow the leaf.

4.4 Cat's Ear (Hypochaeris radicata)

Common Name: Flatweed, Cat's Ear, False Dandelion

Description: The leaves of the Cat's Ear are low-lying and lobed, with a surface covered in numerous fine hairs. The leaves grow to an average length of eight inches and are arranged in a rosette around the main taproot of the plant. From these leaves rise tall stems, forked, that carry large, yellow blooms that mature to form seeds that are similar to that of a dandelion.

Distinguishing Features: All the plants exude a milk-like secretion when cut into.

Location: The Cat's Ear thrives throughout North America, especially in sunny areas. It likes to flourish in soils that have been disturbed. To forage for it, search along the road, remember the rules for this, yards, parks (remember the precautions), and livestock pastures.

Seasonality: It grows from the onset of springtime to winter. It is difficult to forage for this plant in the summers. In a snowy area, the cat's ear first appears on the onset of spring, and disappears once frost begins to appear.

Harvest: A good pair of scissors or garden shears are used to snip off the leaves. A trowel may be used to harvest the taproot of the plant.

Flavor Profile: The leaves of the cat's ear are quite bland and are ideal for a salad. The roots carry a mildly bland flavor.

Edible Parts: You may safely consume the new buds, flowers, the new shoots, the taproots and the leaves.

Serving Suggestions and Other Culinary Applications: The leaves may be used in raw applications or cooked as you would greens. The taproot, when ground, makes a great replacement for coffee with the bonus that it is caffeine-free.

Precautions: This plant is considered as a weed by many gardeners, hence take precautions as the plant you may encounter might have been sprayed with a weed killer. To be safe, gather only in areas that are guaranteed to not have been touched by humans.

4.5 CATTAIL (TYPHA LATIFOLIA)

Common Name: Punks, Corn Dog Grass, Bulrush, Cat tail, Cat o' Nine Tail.

Description: The cattail possesses a long slender stalk with equally slender leaves that surround the stalk. The stalks themselves form an anchor for the brown seed heads which later ripen and get blown away at the end of the summer. The flowers blossom in the springtime once more and for a brief period, you can find the bright yellow pollen at the tips of each flower. The plant has no other plants that are similar to it in appearance.

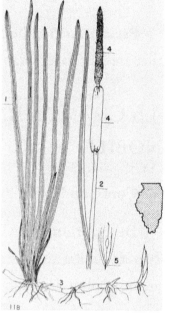

Distinguishing Features: The cattails are a wetland plant and are best found there due to their distinctive profile.

Location: The cattail may be found in the North American wetlands, and even alongside ponds, or bodies of water that are still or even slow in their currents. It prefers a muddy soil that can retain moisture throughout the entire year.

Seasonality: The cattail may gathered throughout the year, and is ideal for foragers and survivalists. The shoots are best harvested early in the springtime. The pollen is best harvested in the late portions of springtime.

Harvest: A sharp knife may be used to harvest the young, green shoots in the springtime and the flowers while still green. The Cattail Rhizome can cause a mess when you harvest it, so dig carefully. To harvest the pollen, use a large zip-lock bag to catch the pollen from when you shake the stalks into the bag.

Flavor Profile: The type of flavor varies in accordance with the plant part that is used. The shoots of the cattail are reminiscent of asparagus whereas the rhizome can be quite bland and starchy in texture. The pollen adds a different flavor when used in baked items.

Edible Parts: The pollen, the flowers, the rhizomes and the young shoots may be safely consumed.

Serving Suggestions and Other Culinary Applications: The young shoots may be eaten raw, or cooked as you would asparagus. Remove the sheathe from the cattail flowers before you prepare them for consumption. These are best boiled as you would a corn cob and eaten as such. The rhizome of the cattail is best used when it has been boiled or baked but can be safely consumed raw especially in emergencies.

Precautions: If the cattail is found in polluted water, it may absorb all the toxins and chemicals that are sent to its rhizome. Forage only in areas that are not polluted.

4.6 CHAMOMILE (MATRICARIA CHAMOMILE; CHAMAEMELUM NOBILE)

Common Name: Pineapple Weed, Chamomile, Camomile

Description: The Chamomile has tiny white flowers with bright yellow centers similar to that of a miniature daisy. The leaves of the Chamomile are quite abundant and resemble a fern in their shape. The plant may reach a maximum height of three feet and has a flowering season that spans from May to October, though this is dependent on its locale.

Distinguishing Features: The Chamomile has several stalks that grow from the root. These stalks tend to spread and create branches which can make the Chamomile quite large.

Location: The Chamomile may be found throughout North America, where it prefers open locations that receive a lot of sun exposure, with little shade. It prefers to thrive in meadows, pastures, old gardens and roadsides (remember the rules for roadside foraging) as a result.

Seasonality: It is a springtime plant that disappears once the first frosts of winter sets in. It can be found all year in warm climates.

Harvest: A sharp pair of scissors or garden shears may be used to snip off the stems and flowers of the Chamomile.

Flavor Profile: Chamomile is often associated in medicine as an herbal plant and its flavor is reflective of its use as an herbal tea. This herbal flavor also suits in raw applications, and its flowers, when used in salads, evoke a taste similar to that of apples.

Edible Parts: You may safely use the buds, the matured flowers and the leaves.

Serving Suggestions and Other Culinary Applications: Chamomile is ideally enjoyed in its raw state, and you may steep the flowers for a medicinal tea that serves to calm you down. The leaves may be steamed for a few minutes to make a tasty side dish.

Precautions: Pregnant women should not consume Chamomile in any form as this can induce uterine contractions that may lead to a miscarriage. Additionally, if you are allergic to ragweed, you may also be allergic to chamomile.

4.7 CHICKWEED (STELLARIA MEDIA)

Common Name: Satin flower, star weed, birdseed, starwort, chickweed, winter weed, tongue grass, craches, maruns.

Description: The chickweed is a creeper that reaches a maximum height of eight inches tall. It has the tendency to form small mats that have an area of sixteen inches. The leaves themselves are small, which range from a half inch to an inch in length, are arranged in pairs. The leaves of the chickweed are egg shaped with a smooth edge and a pointed tip. The minuscule white blossoms possess five deep-cleft petals supported by a long green sepal.

Distinguishing Features: The blooms of the chickweed are tightly clustered at the end of its stems.

Location: The plant may be found all over North America in areas that receive a lot of sun exposure, and in areas that receive partial shade.

Seasonality: The chickweed is able to grow all year and thrives when it has no shade. Though it is abundant in the summer, it peaks in flavor towards the late months of fall to the early onset of spring. The plant may also be foraged in the winter when the snow thaws.

Harvest: A pair of scissors or garden shears may be used to snip the chickweed. When you do so, gently bunch up the runners before you snip them away. Cut one to two inches only from the ground (remember the section on ethical harvesting).

Flavor Profile: In its raw state, chickweed has a light, sweet flavor that resembles corn. Once it has been cooked, it tastes like spinach.

Edible Parts: You may safely consume the leaves, stems, the flowers and its buds.

Serving Suggestions and Other Culinary Applications: Wash the chickweed before you consume it. The chopped plants are best suited for salads, though if left whole, make for an interesting design on your plates. The edible parts may be eaten raw or cooked, though be advised that when you cook chickweed, it shrinks so you would have to properly portion the amount that you intend to consume.

Precautions: The plant is similar to toxic spotted spurge, though it has differently shaped flowers and exudes a milky sap if cut. Knotweed is another plant that is similar in appearance to chickweed, but its leaves are arranged alternately along the stems, rather than in pairs like the chickweed.

4.8 CHICORY (CICHORIUM INTYBUS)

Common Name: Succory, Barbe de Capucin, Chicory, Hendibeh, Wild Succory

Description: The Chicory is a very attractive plant with its sky-blue blossoms that have the approximate size of a quarter. The plant can grow to a height of three feet tall at the most, with small leaves arrayed along its stalks and clustered leaves that resemble a dandelion at its base.

Distinguishing Features: The leaves of the chicory are hirsute, attached to a tough and woody stem. While the plant is known for its sky-blue blossoms, they may also be pink, white or pale purple in color. The flowers open early in the morning and close in the afternoon.

Location: The Chicory may be found throughout North America, and found along the sides of the road, in the sites of old barns, livestock pastures and areas where the soil has undergone disturbance.

Seasonality: The young chicory leaves are best collected in March and November, when they are new. The intense heat has the tendency to concentrate the bitter taste. The chicory shoots are best harvested in the springtime. If you cultivate your own chicory, it is possible to blanch the shoots with the use of an upside-down flowerpot to cover them a few weeks before you intend to harvest. This results in shoots that have a mildly bitter flavor, and a softer shoot. The large roots for roasting may be harvested from the late part of summer to late fall.

Harvest: The roots may be harvested with the use of a small, sharp trowel. Use a small knife to cut up the shoots.

Flavor Profile: Once it has been roasted, the root of the chicory has a smooth and pleasant taste that makes it an excellent coffee substitute – as popularized by the Café du Monde in New Orleans. The shoots of the chicory have a mild bitter taste that can add dimensions of flavor to salads and other dishes with cooked greens. The root may be eaten once it has been boiled until tender with a flavor similar to that of a parsnip.

Edible Parts: All the parts of the chicory are edible, but the most prized parts by foragers are the young shoots and roots. The buds of the chicory flowers are also used in salads.

Serving Suggestions and Other Culinary Applications: You may eat the chicory shoots either raw or cooked. To cook the root, you may boil, bake or roast it to prevent the build-up of excess gas in your body once you consume it. In emergencies, you may eat the harvested root raw as it makes for a great protein source. Medicinally, it is a great antihelminthic and reduces the incidence of infestations in livestock who graze upon it.

Precautions: Chicory may be inadvertently sprayed upon with insecticides and weed killers. Take precautions when you harvest from populated areas. To be safe, harvest the chicory in areas that are guaranteed to be free from the effects of these sprays.

4.9 COMMON MALLOW (MALVA NEGLECTA)

Common Name: Pancake plant, common mallow, cheeseweed, cheeses

Description: The Common Mallow grows low to the ground with leaves that are rounded in shape, with serrated edges. The leaves are fanned out around the base of the stem. Its flowers have five-petals that range in color from pale lavender to white that surround a center that is pale in color. Once the flowers have withered, the plant produces flat, green fruit.

Distinguishing Features: The flowers have striped petals and the profile of the flower is similar to that of a hibiscus.

Location: The plant flourishes throughout North America and can grow in myriad locations. It prefers to thrives alongside paths and sidewalks, as well as parks, livestock pastures, and lawns though you would need to exercise caution with the latter three areas for instances of spraying. The common mallow thrives in soil that has been tilled and grows along fences, walls and curbs.

Seasonality: The common mallow can be found all-year, but it is ideally foraged in the springtime and autumn when it produces it young shoots.

Harvest: Gently pluck the blossoms, buds and fruits from the stems. Use a pair of scissors to snip the leaves from the plant.

Flavor Profile: The flavors of the common mallow are mild, yet appeal to the forager.

Edible Parts: You may safely consume the buds, flowers, leaves and its green fruit.

Serving Suggestions and Other Culinary Applications: You may use the fruits and flowers in raw applications. The fruits may be sautéed in other preparations. The leaves must be cooked before they are consumed as they are quite chewy when raw. Simply steam or sauté the leaves before you add them to a dish. You may dry the leaves to make a medicinal herbal tea. Similar to arrowroot, you may use mallow to thicken stews, soups and potages.

Precautions: Mallow can be a laxative, especially if consumed in large quantities. Be especially aware of the laxative effect if you consume a lot of the common mallow.

4.10 CURLY DOCK (RULEX CRISPUS)

Common Name: Yellow Dock, Narrowdock, Sour Dock, Curly Dock, Coffeeweed

Description: The Curly Dock possess a robust taproot that is surrounded by long, tapered foliage with a rippled edge. The flower-bearing portions are supported by long stalks on which narrow leaves are arrayed alternately from its center, these arise in the late spring. Once matured, the leaves of the curly dock assume a rubescent hue, while clusters of tiny green blooms appear at the apex of the stem. They later give way to small brown seeds.

Distinguishing Features: The blossoms of the Curly Dock resemble burrs and are just as sticky. Take caution as they may be quite finicky to remove and will readily attach to pant legs and animal fur.

Location: You may find the Curly Dock throughout North America and it is considered by the general population to be invasive. You may forage for the plant in open fields, the sides of the road, and in areas where the soil has undergone some form of disturbance.

Seasonality: This plant is best foraged in the early spring before the central stem begins to sprout.

Harvest: Simply use a sharp knife to cut the young leaves from the rest of the plant.

Flavor Profile: The young leaves of the curly dock possess a sharp, yet bright flavor. Once the leaves begin to mature, the leaves begin to take on a bitter flavor, and become very chewy. This renders the plant unpalatable.

Edible Parts: The young leaves of the curly dock are the most edible parts of the plant, though you may safely consume the stems and its seeds. If you intend to consume the stems, it is necessary to peel before you eat.

Serving Suggestions and Other Culinary Applications: The plant contains a large amount of a compound called oxalic acid – the same acid that is present in rhubarb. You may safely consume the young leaves in raw applications such as salads, but be sure to do so in moderation. To be safe, you may boil the greens before you consume them. If the leaves retain their bitterness, be sure to

change the water before you boil again. The seeds of the curly dock may be ground and used as a substitute for coffee. The same seeds may be ground into a flour that resembles buckwheat.

Precautions: Always wash the plant before you taste it as its leaves contain a natural astringent that can numb your tongue and irritate it.

4.11 DANDELION (TARAXACUM)

Common Name: Peasant's Clock, Witches' Gowan, Milk Witch, Gowan, Downhead, Dandelion, Canker Root, Blowball.

Description: The Dandelion is characterized by its broad, verdant leaves that cluster close to the ground. There is a single stem that rises up from this cluster, that secrets a milky sap. The stem supports a bright yellow bloom that has a scent similar to honey. The familiar downy seed-head appears once the flower has faded.

Distinguishing Features: The Dandelion is a plant that is able to return and thrive in the same place even though you and other foragers have harvested it from the roots up.

Location: Dandelions are found all over North America, and are very common. They thrive the most in lawns that have not been chemically treated, in the pasturelands, parklands, and the sites of old houses.

Seasonality: Dandelions prefer a warmer climate and will be available all year round in these places. In a cooler climate, the dandelion shoots begin to appear once the soil begins to take on warmth. You may gather the small dandelion shoots once they begin to sprout.

Harvest: You may simply pluck the small buds, leaves, and flowers from the dandelion plant. If the soil is soft, you may also harvest the dandelion root with ease. In firmer soils, use a trowel to carefully harvest the roots. Soak the roots for at least a quarter of an hour to ensure you can clean it up easily.

Flavor Profile: The buds and blossoms of the Dandelion carry a light floral flavor that carries a hint of sweetness. The younger shoots carry a bitter taste that gets reduced once it has been cooked

down. The flavor of the dandelion peaks before the flower begins to bloom. The dandelion root has a bitter flavor that becomes reduced once fall sets in.

Edible Parts: You may safely forage for the young leaves, buds, flowers and roots. The older leaves are very bitter. You cannot eat the stalk.

Serving Suggestions and Other Culinary Applications: Be sure to wash every part of the dandelion before you eat. Greens, buds and flowers may be served in raw applications or added to other recipes. The Dandelion root should be washed, scrubbed, peeled and cooked before consumption. The root may also be roasted and ground to substitute for coffee. The Dandelion may be used to make a tea that would reduce your uric acid levels in your blood. To do this, the plant may be eaten raw or pureed into a juice as well.

Precautions: The Dandelion is considered by many gardeners to be a weed, and may have been sprayed on. Take note of the precautions for foraging in areas that may have undergone chemical treatment with weed killers and herbicides. Forage for the plant only where the Dandelion could not have been sprayed upon.

4.12 ELDER (SAMBUCUS NIGRA)

Common Name: Elderberry, Elder

Description: The deciduous Elder resembles a small shrub or a smaller tree that reaches up to thirty feet in height. The broad, vibrant green foliage of the elder are arranged in opposite pairs. The tiny five-petal blooms range in color from white to cream and yields glossy, purple berries.

Distinguishing Features: The blossoms and berries of the elder grow in tight clusters. The bark of the tree has a light gray coloration which develops vertical furrows as the plant matures.

Location: The tree may be found all over North America and will thrive in damp soil, or soil that is dry, yet fertile. The tree prefers sunny locales.

Seasonality: The blossoms of the Elder Tree bloom towards the end of springtime, and the resultant berries are ripened towards the end of summer and the start of fall.

Harvest: A pair of scissors or garden shears may be used to carefully snip away the blossoms from the Elder Tree. You may pick the berries by hand.

Flavor Profile: The blooms of the Elder tree carry a flavor like honey and are sweet. The ripened berries are sweet, with an undertone reminiscent of astringents that disappear once the berries are cooked.

Edible Parts: You may safely consume the berries and flowers.

Serving Suggestions and Other Culinary Applications: The blossoms and berries are well suited for tea, and may also be fermented into wines and cordials. The berries are ideal for jams, jellies and syrups. Elderflower tea is able to ease congestion and is easily made when you steep the dried flowers in water for 15 minutes to infuse properly.

Precautions: The unripe elder berries are very toxic, which may remain once the berry ripens. Be sure to cook the berries as cooking eliminates the toxin from the berries.

4.13 FIDDLEHEAD FERN (MATTEUCCIA STRUTHIOPTERIS)

Common Name: Shuttlecock Fern, Ostrich Fern, Fiddlehead Fern

Description: The fiddlehead fern is a familiar sight to many foragers due to its distinctively shaped fronds. The crown-shaped growths produce two different structures, with some that are tall and leafy, while the other fronds are shorter in height, with a woody, brown stalk.

Distinguishing Features: The fiddlehead fern obtains its name due to the tightly furled tops that resemble the head of a fiddle, or that of a violin.

Location: You may forage for the fiddleheads in the cool, temperate areas of North America where it thrives in woodland areas.

Seasonality: The fiddlehead ferns begin to emerge in the early months of spring and remain in their areas for a maximum of three days. In other locales, the fiddleheads may sprout in the months of April and May.

Harvest: Simply use a sharp knife to carefully cut away the young fiddleheads.

Flavor Profile: The flavor of the fiddlehead ferns are similar to that of the asparagus and sugar snap peas, while its fronds retain a crisp texture.

Edible Parts: The only edible parts of the fiddlehead ferns are the young fronds as they are quite tender. The more matured fronds are inedible due to their chewiness.

Serving Suggestions and Other Culinary Applications: These harvested fiddlehead fronds are best steamed or sautéed to bring out the most of their flavor and increase their tenderness. This has made them quite popular among locavores where the fiddlehead fern can be easily foraged.

Precautions: There are a lot of edible fern species in North America, as well as other inedible species. Caution must be taken to only forage for the species that are edible. Fiddlehead ferns may be protected by foraging laws in some areas due to their rarity, so you would have to check that you can safely forage for them in your local area.

4.14 GARLIC MUSTARD (ALLIARIA PETIOLATA)

Common Name: Poor Man's Mustard, Garlic Root, Garlic Mustard, Jack-by-the-Hedge, Hedge Garlic, Penny Hedge

Description: The Garlic Mustard is a biennial plant that may be consumed in its first or second year. While it is in its first year of growth, the plant sprouts a cluster of round, wrinkled leaves that are similar to those produced by violets. A year after, the stalks of the plant grow taller and produce white, cross-shaped blossoms.

Distinguishing Features: Once the leaves have been crushed between your fingers, they exude an aroma similar to garlic, hence its name.

Location: The plant may be found throughout North America especially in areas where the soil has undergone some type of disturbance. It thrives along the fringes of the forests, in livestock pastures and open meadows. It also thrives in areas that have rich and moist soils with a lot of shady areas, and can thrive in forests. The plant is a spreader and tends to grow in large patches.

Seasonality: The plant reaches its peak at the later autumn months when its base leaves begin to make their first appearance. It is also best foraged in the early spring before the stalk that supports its flowers begins to sprout.

Harvest: The plant is considered to be an invasive species and it is best to simply uproot the plant from the ground, though do so carefully.

Flavor Profile: The garlic mustard plant has a sharp, herbaceous flavor that can be mildly bitter. Most foragers do however find the mild bitterness to be pleasant.

Edible Parts: You may safely consume the young, tender leaves as these are the best part of the plant. The older leaves and other parts, while they are not toxic, tend to have a bitter taste that many find unpalatable.

Serving Suggestions and Other Culinary Applications: You may separate the leaves from the root base and wash well to remove any soil from it. You may add the leaves to a salad if you enjoy the mild bitter flavor and herbal undertones it has, otherwise you can steam or blanch it before you eat it as a side dish. The plant may be used as a dye to turn objects yellow.

Precautions: If you intend to cultivate a wild plant garden, it is best that you leave out the garlic mustard as it can easily take over your entire garden. The plant is ideal if you forage for it in the wilds.

4.15 JERUSALEM ARTICHOKE (SUNCHOKES) (HELIANTHUS TUBEROSUS)

Common Name: Sunchoke, Jerusalem Artichoke, Topinambour

Description: the plant of the Jerusalem Artichoke resembles that of a sunflower in its miniature form, from which it derives its name. The Jerusalem artichoke has no relationship with that of Jerusalem, but from a corrupted form of *girasole,* which means sunflower in Italian. You can expect then that the blossoms of the plant have a brown center surrounded by sunshine yellow petals. The stems of the plant are quite slender and have a slight coating of hair with soft leaves. The "choke" of the plant are gnarled and have an uneven surface and closely resemble the rhizome of a ginger.

Distinguishing Features: Once matured, the Jerusalem artichoke can reach up to six feet in height, and produces several blossoms from one plant, unlike other sunflowers.

Location: You may find the sunchoke all over North America where it prefers any type of soil, as long as the area it is in has a lot of sun exposure. They thrive along the sides of the road and inside vacant lots, as well as in fields left to fallow, and in the sites of old homes.

Seasonality: They are at their best, and are edible only after the first frost while the plant still has some foliage.

Harvest: Carefully dig around the plant to harvest the roots, that you may not disturb the plants around it.

Flavor Profile: The root of the Jerusalem artichoke has a taste that evokes that of an artichoke and are generally mild and pleasant once they have been foraged for once the first frost has set in. If foraged earlier than this time, they are quite unpalatable.

Edible Parts: The chokes are the only edible parts of the Jerusalem artichoke.

Serving Suggestions and Other Culinary Applications: You may consume the choke raw, as long as it has been carefully washed, as it contributes a crisp, textural element if tossed into salads. They are best steamed, rather than boiled as the latter method tends to reduce the choke into a mush. Steam allows you to keep the flavor and their shape intact and makes it a great side dish for braised dishes. If roasted and ground, the choke makes for a great coffee substitute.

Precautions: Do not harvest the choke of the plant earlier than the first frost as the choke will have high concentrations of inulin, a compound that can cause you to bloat, and your stomach to have gastric distress, and excessive flatulence. This compound only dissipates once the plant has fully matured.

4.16 JUNIPER (JUNIPERUS COMMUNIS)

Common Name: Juniper, Common juniper

Description: The Juniper is a coniferous evergreen that can reach a maximum height of up to thirty feet tall. It may also take the form of a shrub. Once fully ripened, the female seed cones or the berries of the juniper develop a waxy exterior and become a blue-black color. The male cones are quite small and yellow and simply detach from the plant once it has dispersed its pollen.

Distinguishing Features: The foliage of the juniper tree grow in whorls of three leaves or needles

Location: The juniper is quite common and is widespread all over North America, particularly in the cooler northern climates where it thrives the most. It is also present in many homes as a cultivated ornamental tree.

Seasonality: The tree ripens over a period of three years where the blossoms of the juniper bloom in the first year of the cycle. The blossoms then yield green berries in the second year of the cycle before the berries ripen in the third year of the cycle. The juniper may have all three cycles present in a single tree at one time so be sure to harvest only the ripened berries.

Harvest: Simply pluck the ripened berries from the tree with your fingers.

Flavor Profile: The juniper has a cool flavor, known to be refreshing as it evokes the flavor of an evergreen.

Edible Parts: You may only harvest the ripened berries, purple in their coloration.

Serving Suggestions and Other Culinary Applications: The berries of the juniper are well known as the flavor of gin. Because of their pungency, they may be crushed and used to flavor other foods. The sap and inner bark of the juniper are used by Native American tribes as a form of sweetener.

Precautions: The juniper has several species that are inedible, so be sure that you forage only from the common juniper.

4.17 Lamb's Quarters (Chenopodium album)

Common Name: Goosefoot, Fat Hen, Pigweed, Lamb's Quarters, Wild Spinach

Description: The plant has central stalks that range in color from green to reddish-green that later take on a woody texture as the plant further matures. The leaves are shaped like arrowheads and have a soft texture, with a slightly silvery center and serrated edges. The plant reaches a height of four to six feet.

Distinguishing Features: The lamb's quarters are often found in large masses, their silvery leaves are distinctive enough to identify them.

Location: The Lamb's Quarters are a resilient species found all over North America, and thrive along the sides of the road, within gardens and construction sites, in the pasturelands and in areas where the soil has undergone some form of disturbance.

Seasonality: The plant may be found all year round in warm climates, but in temperate zones; the plant emerges in the springtime and dies once the first frosts have set in.

Harvest: Use a pair of scissors or sharp garden shears to snip off the stems of the plant. Leaves should only be harvested from the top of the plant.

Flavor Profile: The plant has an earthy flavor, reminiscent to that of matured spinach or chard. The mineral like flavor is a result of its high calcium concentration.

Edible Parts: You may safely consume the leaves and stems only.

Serving Suggestions and Other Culinary Applications: The young leaves of the lamb's quarters and its smaller stems are ideal for raw applications, as the matured leaves can be quite bitter. Boil the leaves to improve their taste but be warned of the shrinkage, so be sure to cook more than you need. You may make an infusion from the leaves of the lamb's quarters to form a tea to soothe diarrhea.

Precautions: Only harvest the plant from areas where the plant has not been sprayed with any herbicide, weed killer or any form of chemical.

4.18 MILKWEED (ASCLEPIAS SYRIACA)

Common Name: Silkweed, Milkweed

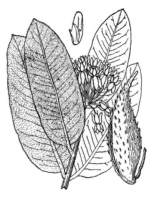

Description: The foliage of the Milkweed are broad, thick and have a smooth edge. The tightly packed buds unfurl into clusters of fragrant blossoms that later give way to seed pods. These seed pods begin to ripen fully, late into the summer, where they burst open to release seeds that resemble parachutes. Once matured, the plant reaches a maximum height of four feet tall.

Distinguishing Features: The edible species of milkweed present with fine white hairs layered on their stems.

Location: The milkweed is found all over North America where it thrives in open locations that have a lot of sun exposure. It is also easily foraged for along the sides of the roads, in the pasturelands, and in the meadows.

Seasonality: Harvest the young milkweed shoots in the spring, while the ripened pods are best in the late summer months.

Harvest: The young shoots may be picked or carefully snipped in the early months of spring, and look for the youngest leaves as they are the tenderest at this time. Carefully pluck the buds and ripened pods from the tops of the plant.

Flavor Profile: The flavor of the milkweed resembles a hybrid of green beans and asparagus. The more mature versions of the plant tend to have a bitter taste that verges on the unpalatable.

Edible Parts: You may safely foraged for the buds, shoots and the ripened milkweed pods.

Serving Suggestions and Other Culinary Applications: All the edible parts of the milkweed may be eaten raw, or steamed, boiled, baked or sautéed in other applications.

Precautions: You may cultivate the plant as it makes an excellent pollinator for the rest of your plants. It can cause dermatitis in individuals with sensitive skin, and may induce latex allergies in those who are allergic to latex of which it is a source. Toxic dogbane is a related species which is similar in appearance to milkweed, save the fine white hairs on its stems. The plant may blister the skin.

4.19 NETTLE (URTICA DIOICA)

Common Name: Common nettle, burn hazel, stinging nettle, burn weed, nettle, burn nettle.

Description: The perennial nettle has an herbaceous structure that can reach heights of three to seven feet once it matures. The soft, verdant foliage may reach up to six inches in length with blossoms that can be green, yellow or brown in color.

Distinguishing Features: The nettle plant prefers thrive in large patches.

Location: You may forage for the nettle all over the temperate zones of North America where it prefers to thrive in areas that become shady for a few hours each day. They tend to propagate in the same areas yearly, where they prefer rich soils that have undergone human or animal disturbance, the woodlands with moist soils, and along the sides of trails that receive the shade that it needs.

Seasonality: The younger nettle shoots begin to emerge in the early months of spring once snow begins to thaw, and disappear once winter begins to set in. The plant is able to propagate itself, and thus it is possible to forage for its leaves from the start of spring to the late autumn months. Forage for the leaves before the nettle plant blooms, preferably in the early months of spring or in autumn.

Harvest: Gently pluck the leaves from the plants. Avoid nettles that have flowered as the leaves of this plant have taken on a bitter flavor and are very tough.

Flavor Profile: The nettles contribute a pleasant, earthy flavor where its leaves bear a flavor reminiscent to that of cucumber and spinach.

Edible Parts: You may safely forage for the young nettle leaves. Larger leaves may be consumed with care.

Serving Suggestions and Other Culinary Applications: They cannot be eaten raw and have to be cooked before eaten. Prepare them as you would spinach leaves and are best sautéed, boiled, or even steamed. The leaves may be used as a compress to relieve arthritis and muscle pain.

Precautions: Once matured, the nettle takes on the stinging, hollow fibers it is known for, and may cause instances of severe itchiness and urticaria. Wear protective clothing such as long pants, long sleeves, and gloves if you intend to forage for nettles.

4.20 Nipplewort (Lapsana communis)

Common Name: Nipplewort

Description: The plant has clustered leaves located at its base, with spindle-like stems that are covered in many fine hairs. It has yellow blossoms that can span up to an inch across. The plant can reach a height of up to three feet.

Distinguishing Features: The buds of the plant are elongated in shape and are striped in dark green.

Location: You may find nipplewort almost everywhere in North America as it is a common plant. It prefers to thrive in soils that have undergone some form of disturbance.

Seasonality: The young leaves of the plant are best foraged in the springtime and early autumn months.

Harvest: Carefully pluck the young leaves from the base of the plant.

Flavor Profile: The young leaves taste similar to spinach, though once matured, they take on a spicy flavor similar to that of radish. Once the leaves are older, the flavor becomes bitter and unpalatable.

Edible Parts: The young leaves of the plant are best for foragers. You may consume the matured leaves, but they must be boiled first to remove the bitter taste.

Serving Suggestions and Other Culinary Applications: The younger leaves are best used in raw applications such as salads. They may also be sautéed, steamed or boiled as you would spinach.

Precautions: The plant makes for a great pollinator but is considered to be a weed by many. As a result, areas where it grows may have been treated with herbicide and caution should be taken to forage in areas where no such treatment has been applied.

4.21 Nipplewort Prickly Pear Cactus (Opuntia humifusa)

Common Name: Tuna, Prickly Pear Cactus, Paddle Cactus, Nopales

Description: This is a common type of cactus that has flat and jointed cactus pads with yellow flowers that later develop into fruits of a dull red color.

Distinguishing Features: The spines of the prickly pear are arranged in tufts rather than as individual spikes like other cacti.

Location: The plant may be found throughout North America where it prefers to thrive in desert locales with numerous sand dunes. It also prefers to thrive in rocky and mountainous slopes. The plant prefers soils that are dry and rocky with a high amount of sand.

Seasonality: The young pads are best foraged for in the spring months where the spines are still small and undeveloped. The fruits are best foraged in the early summer months to the late fall months.

Harvest: To harvest, it is best if you leave the base pad in its entirety and harvest only the small pads that are located farthest from this base pad. Remember to follow the ethical harvesting rule on two thirds when you harvest the fruit of the prickly pear.

Flavor Profile: The young cactus plants have a taste that resembles the green bean. The fruits however are lightly sweet and have a refreshing quality.

Edible Parts: You may safely forage for the fruits and young pads.

Serving Suggestions and Other Culinary Applications: To prepare the pads and fruits for consumption, peel off the tough, outer skin to access the inner layer that you can eat. The pads require cooking and are best when pickled. You may consume the fruit raw or cook it as you would fruit. Poultices made from the flesh are used to enhance the healing process for wounds.

Precautions: Take the necessary precautions to protect yourself from the spines of the prickly pear. Be sure to inspect yourself for ticks as they tend to hide among the pads of the plant.

4.22 Nipplewort Purslane (Portulaca oleracea)

Common Name: Moss Rose, Little Hogweed, Pursley, Purslane, Pigweed, Verdolaga, Pussley

Description: The leaves of the purslane are oval-shaped and succulent attached to smooth stems that are reddish in hue. Its small, yellow blossoms have five petals.

Distinguishing Features: The plant grows in a straggly bunch that spreads. The flowers open in the morning only if it is sunny, and close before noontime.

Location: You may forage for pigweed all over North America where it prefers rich soils in sunny locations. It may also be found along the side of the roads and trails, and may grow in the cracks of sidewalks and in waste areas (though the latter two are not advised for foraging due to the potential for chemical contamination).

Seasonality: The plant flourishes from the early months of spring to late autumn.

Harvest: To harvest, simply snip the pigweed from the mature plant with a pair of scissors or garden shears. Leave up to two inches of the plant growth near the roots that it can replenish itself.

Flavor Profile: The leaves possess a salty, citrusy taste reminiscent of lemons and is coveted by many foragers.

Edible Parts: You may safely forage for the leaves, stems, flowers, tips and seeds.

Serving Suggestions and Other Culinary Applications: You may add the purslane to salads, though you may also boil it, sauté, steam or bake the plant if desired. It is also used to treat headaches and a variety of digestive disorders.

Precautions: Forage only in areas where no herbicide has been used to eliminate the purslane.

4.23 Nipplewort Ramps (Allium tricoccum)

Common Name: Wild Leeks, Ramps

Description: Ramps produce two to three light green leaves that range from half a foot to a foot in length. The leaves have parallel veins and are quite soft in texture, they rise out from a bulb, similar to how the leaves come from a scallion. If the plant is bruised or tasted, the aroma is evocative of onions. It produces a flower that only appears once the green leaves have yellowed and withered.

Distinguishing Features: You cannot miss the soft, flat green leaves that exude an onion like aroma when pinched.

Location: You may forage for ramps throughout the eastern and central portions of North America, as it prefers the more temperate zones in the continent.

Seasonality: They are best found from the early part of April to the early part of May.

Harvest: You may simply harvest the plant in its entirety with care not to disturb the surrounding plants.

Flavor Profile: The flavor of ramps resembles that of onions, where it has led to the ramp as a coveted ingredient by many restaurants.

Edible Parts: The bulb and the soft green leaves may be used in a variety of culinary applications.

Serving Suggestions and Other Culinary Applications: Use the bulb as you would an onion, while the leaves may be blanched or sautéed to add additional flavor to a dish, or to wrap around a dish.

Precautions: Lily of the valley looks similar to ramps, except that its leaves do not exude the onion like aroma that ramps have. Take caution as Lily of the Valley is poisonous.

4.24 Nipplewort Sheep Sorrel (Rumex acetosella)

Common Name: Sour Weed, Red Sorrel, Field Sorrel, Sheep Sorrel

Description: The plant has green foliage that resemble miniature arrowheads in shape. The red tinged stems possess deep ridges. The blossoms of the plant are colored like wine.

Distinguishing Features: The plant has tall, erect stems, and may reach a maximum height of one and a half feet tall.

Location: Sheep Sorrel is considered to be an invasive plant found throughout North America. It prefers to thrive along the pasturelands, parklands, and meadowlands and will grow alongside the roads and trails. It prefers to flourish in areas that receive a lot of sun exposure.

Seasonality: The young leaves of the sheep sorrel may be harvested in the early months of spring, while the larger leaves of the sorrel may be foraged once the later days of summer commence.

Harvest: You may gently pluck the leaves from the plant, or simply harvest the entire plant for later preservation.

Flavor Profile: Young leaves of the Sheep Sorrel possess a tangy flavor. Older leaves have a stronger, more intense sour flavor.

Edible Parts: The whole plant is edible though many foragers find only the leaves palatable enough for consumption.

Serving Suggestions and Other Culinary Applications: You may use the young leaves in raw applications such as salads; it is also ideal when steamed, sautéed, baked or boiled as it makes a great supplementary ingredient in many casseroles. The leaves may be steeped to make an infusion used to treat diarrhea.

Precautions: Because the plant is considered as an invasive species, it may be treated with herbicides and thus, you should only forage for this plant in places that you are certain have not been chemically treated.

4.25 Nipplewort Shepherd's Purse (Capsella bursa-pastoris)

Common Name: Shepherd's purse

Description: The triangular sheep-pods of the Shepherd's purse are arrayed along the stem of the plant. The leaves that are located at the base of the plant closely resemble that of the dandelion.

Distinguishing Features: The plant produces a distinct cluster of small, white blossoms that have four petals.

Location: You may find the Shepherd's Purse all over North America as it is a resilient plant that can thrive in any location that receives a lot of sun.

Seasonality: You may forage for the plant from the early days of springtime to the late days of fall. In warmer climates however, you may forage for it throughout the entire year.

Harvest: Carefully dig around the plant to harvest its roots, and gently pluck the leaves from the plant following the two-thirds rule. You may safely harvest the entire plant should you choose to do so.

Flavor Profile: Once boiled, the leaves of the plant are similar in flavor to cabbage, though while raw it has a flavor and scent reminiscent to that of turnips. The matured, older leaves and its seedpods retain a flavor similar to pepper. The root of the plant shares the same spiciness associated with ginger root.

Edible Parts: You may safely forage for the leaves, shoots, seedpods and roots.

Serving Suggestions and Other Culinary Applications: The young leaves of the shepherd's purse are great in raw applications and may be tossed in salads. The matured leaves provide their best flavor once they have been cooked. You may toast the seeds of the plant and grind them. The roots may be eaten in their raw state, or you may choose to roast them. An infusion made from the leaves of the shepherd's purse is used to treat a variety of skin disorders.

Precautions: The plant is considered by many to be a weed and may be sprayed with herbicides. Be sure to only forage in areas that have not undergone any form of chemical treatment to ensure you do not ingest the absorbed chemicals.

4.26 NIPPLEWORT SOW THISTLE (SONCHUS OLERACEUS)

Common Name: Hare Thistle, Hare Lettuce, Sow Thistle

Description: The plant has lower leaves that are similar in appearance to the dandelion. Another set of smoother-edged leaves grow higher up on the slender stalk of the sow thistle. Similar to the dandelion, the sow thistle also exudes a viscous sap similar to milk in color.

Distinguishing Features: The blossoms of the sow thistle resemble the flowers of the dandelion, they differ in that the blossoms are colored yellow.

Location: You may forage for the sow thistle all over North America where it prefers wide, open locations that receive a lot of sun exposure. It thrives along the sides of the roads, trails and sunny fields.

Seasonality: Early springtime is an excellent time to forage for the young shoots of the sow thistle. You may continue to forage for these shoots until the late days of summer while the plant still produce blooms.

Harvest: Gently pluck the leaves from the tops of the plant in accordance with the two-thirds rule, you may also sever them from the plant with a knife.

Flavor Profile: The younger leaves of the sow thistle have a relatively mild flavor reminiscent to that of lettuce.

Edible Parts: You may safely forage for the young shoots and leaves of the sow thistle. The stems have to be peeled before you can safely consume them. The latter are not usually consumed as they are generally unpalatable, but in instances of emergencies, they make an excellent emergency source of additional nutrients.

Serving Suggestions and Other Culinary Applications: The young leaves of the sow thistle have a tender texture and are ideal in raw applications such as salads. They are also well suited for

boiled, steamed, and sautéed applications. The sap from the sow thistle is often used to treat cases of warts.

Precautions: Be sure to consume only the smooth sow thistle, as those species with thorns are generally inedible.

4.27 Nipplewort Watercress (Nasturtium officinale)

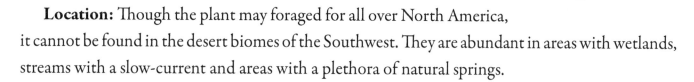

Common Name: Watercress

Description: From the name of the plant, it is a plant that can be either semi-aquatic or aquatic distinguishable due to its bright green foliage, blossoms that are green and white in color, and a hollowed stem that enables it to float on water.

Distinguishing Features: Wild watercress are longer in appearance, as their stems are more spread out compared to the cultivated varieties you may find in your local groceries.

Location: Though the plant may foraged for all over North America, it cannot be found in the desert biomes of the Southwest. They are abundant in areas with wetlands, streams with a slow-current and areas with a plethora of natural springs.

Seasonality: The watercress is best foraged in the springtime.

Harvest: Simply use a pair of scissors or garden shears to gently snip the leaves from the main plant.

Flavor Profile: Watercress is preferred by many chefs as it contributes a spicy flavor, with a tanginess that beautifully offsets numerous dishes.

Edible Parts: The young leaves of the watercress are the most palatable part. Once matured, though they retain their edibility, they are quite bitter and become unpalatable to many foragers and diners.

Serving Suggestions and Other Culinary Applications: Watercress is often eaten raw, where it is made into salads, or as a vegetable in sandwiches. You may also find it used as a garnish for

many restaurant dishes. Its high Vitamin C content makes watercress suitable for the treatment of scurvy, or for anyone who simply wants to boost their immune function.

Precautions: Be sure to only forage for watercress in unpolluted waters as it can readily absorb pollutants that are present in the water. In areas where manure is often used as a fertilizer, the plant may become a source of parasites, and thus should not be foraged from.

4.28 Nipplewort Wild Rose (Rosa arkansana)

Common Name: Wild Prairie Rose, Prairie Rose, Wild Rose

Description: The Wild Rose is a thorny shrub with small, bright green foliage and numerous, fragrant, pink blossoms. Rose hips are produced once the blossoms of the wild rose have withered away.

Distinguishing Features: The blossoms of the wild rose have five petals that surround a bright yellow center.

Location: Though you may forage for the wild rose all over North America, you cannot find it in arid and desert climates. These thrive along the sides of the road, by the fences of properties, in the midst of forests, and along the pathways and gardens of many.

Seasonality: The petals are best foraged in the springtime, while the leaves peak in the springtime and summers. You may forage for the rosehips only in the late summer months.

Harvest: A pair of garden shears may be used to snip the parts that you wish to forage from the plant.

Flavor Profile: The flowers have a characteristic rosy and floral flavor, whereas its foliage retains an herbal quality. The rosehips have a flavor reminiscent to that of berries without the sweetness that is associated with it.

Edible Parts: You may safely forage for the flowers, rosehips and buds. The leaves may be used to make an infusion for tea.

Serving Suggestions and Other Culinary Applications: You may use the flowers, buds and the rosehips in any raw application and they may be consumed as is, provided you wash them

carefully. The rosehip may be made into an infusion for tea, or cooked. The plant finds other applications in cosmetics and candles.

Precautions: Similar to cultivated roses, you can expect that the stems of the wild rose will be thorny, and you should use protective equipment such as gloves when you forage for the plant. They may also be in areas that are treated with pesticides and herbicides, and you should exercise additional caution and only forage in areas where there are no herbicides or pesticides used upon the plants.

4.29 NIPPLEWORT WILD VIOLET (VIOLA ODORATA)

Common Name: Sweet Violet, English Violet, Wild Violet, Garden Violet

Description: The wild violet has the tendency to grow close to the ground in clumps or masses. The foliage is shaped like hearts that funnel downwards into the stems of the plant.

Distinguishing Features: From its name, you can expect that the blossoms of the violet are hued after its namesake color, but they may also present as white, blue or a mixed variation of all three hues.

Location: You may forage for the wild violet in the hills and mountains of North America, where they prefer shady areas. They situate themselves in most parklands, forests, and lawns, and are absent in a flattened and arid terrain.

Seasonality: The wild violets are at their peak when foraged in the early spring months, even before the snow has fully thawed. They may be foraged until the later months of fall. If in a milder climate, you may forage for them all year.

Harvest: Only pick the leaves and flowers in the amounts that you need, in accordance with the guidelines on ethical harvesting.

Flavor Profile: The young foliage of the wild violet retains a mild flavor that becomes bitter as the leaves mature. The flowers are characterized by a sweet flavor.

Edible Parts: You may safely forage the flowers and leaves for consumption.

Serving Suggestions and Other Culinary Applications: The leaves and blossoms of the wild violet may be eaten raw. The foliage may be steamed, boiled and sautéed as you would greens. The roots may be used as a poultice to treat irritations of the skin.

Precautions: Exercise caution when you consume the seeds of the wild violet as excessive consumption can lead to vomiting. Do not eat the seed pods.

4.30 NIPPLEWORT WOOD SORREL (OXALIS ACETOSELLA)

Common Name: Yellow Wood Sorrel, Wood Sorrel, Butterfly Leaves

Description: The three-lobed foliage of the wood sorrel is similar to that of a clover. It grows close to the ground in large clusters.

Distinguishing Features: The minuscule blossoms of the wood sorrel have five petals that range in color from yellow to pink or white.

Location: You may forage for this resilient plant all over North America where it prefers to thrive in gardens, along the trails and in the open meadows and fields. It does well in lawns too. The wood sorrel thrives well in soils that are moist, and in locations that provide a lot of shade.

Seasonality: Wood sorrel is at its most abundant from the early spring months to the late days of fall. You may forage for it all year round in warmer climates.

Harvest: Use a pair of scissors or garden shears to gently snip the portions that you need, or you may just pluck carefully with your fingers the leaves and flowers of the wood sorrel, in accordance with the rule of two-thirds.

Flavor Profile: The wood sorrel contributes a vibrant, citrus flavor to the dishes where it is added to.

Edible Parts: You may safely forage for the flowers, leaves and stems of the wood sorrel.

Serving Suggestions and Other Culinary Applications: Foragers favor the wood sorrel as they may consume it while they forage for other plants. It is also best suited for raw applications. To cook, it may be steamed, sautéed, or boiled as you would other green vegetables. A decoction

made from it is used to treat fevers. The crushed leaves produce an astringent that may be used to cleanse wounds.

Precautions: From the scientific name, you can tell that the wood sorrel contains a high concentration of oxalic acid similar to that of rhubarb. Those with kidney disorders, arthritis, rheumatism, bladder disorders, and gout should not consume wood sorrel as this can cause the formation of oxalic kidney stones.

4.31 YARROW (ACHILLEA MILLEFOLIUM)

Common Name: Thousand Leaf, Thousand Seal, Soldier's Woundwort, Yarrow, Gordaldo, Old Man's Pepper, Devil's Nettle, Plumajillo, Nosebleed Plant

Description: The yarrow has soft-textured leaves with a feathery quality, and white blossoms that grow in a mass on a stem that reaches up to three feet tall.

Distinguishing Features: The plant exudes an aroma that is heavily reminiscent of camphor.

Location: You may forage for yarrow all over North America where it may be found in a variety of elevations from sea level to a maximum elevation of 11,500 feet. It is a resilient plant that is able to flourish in a variety of locations, but prefers open locations with a lot of sun exposure, with well-drained soils.

Seasonality: The plant is at its peak in the springtime to the late summer months. In locales where it may be foraged all year, you may find the young shoots in the early fall months.

Harvest: Gently pluck the amount of leaves that you need from the plant.

Flavor Profile: The yarrow has a lightly sweet flavor with a slightly bitter undertone.

Edible Parts: The young leaves of the yarrow are quite tasty, while its blooms are enjoyed by many foragers. Avoid the older leaves and stems as they retain a bitter and fibrous texture.

Serving Suggestions and Other Culinary Applications: The yarrow provides its best flavor once it has been sautéed, boiled or steamed just like other green vegetables. Its medicinal qualities provide an excellent remedy to staunch wounds and encourage the formation of clots.

Precautions: Forage only in areas where no herbicides have been used on the plant, as yarrow has the tendency to grow alongside plants considered to be weeds.

4.32 YELLOW ROCKET (BARBAREA VULGARIS)

Common Name: Common Cress, Bitter Cress, Land Cress, Indian Posey, Saint Barbara Herb, Yellow Rocket, Upland Cress, Scurvy Cress, Winter Cress

Description: The foliage of the plant grows at its base in long lobes. It possesses a long, fibrous stem with few leaves that produces a cluster of bright yellow blossoms with four petals.

Distinguishing Features: The plant has the tendency to abound in large masses.

Location: You may forage for the plant all over North America, where it prefers to thrive in waste areas (be sure to avoid this), along the sides of the roads and paths, the sides of trails and all over the fields and livestock pastures.

Seasonality: The leaves are at their best when foraged in the early days of spring before the plant flowers. Later days will allow you to forage for the buds that resemble broccoli. It may be foraged all year round in certain climates.

Harvest: You may use your fingers to gently pluck the leaves and the buds from the plant in accordance with your needs and the rules of ethical harvesting.

Flavor Profile: The plant is a species of mustard, and it peaks in flavor in the early days of spring while its leaves bear a flavor reminiscent to that of turnip greens.

Edible Parts: The flowers are not poisonous, but are generally unpalatable. You may safely forage for the young leaves and buds of the plant.

Serving Suggestions and Other Culinary Applications: When consumed in small amounts, yellow rocket produces no effect, but when consumed in excess, it can lead to episodes of flatulence.

The plant is best consumed when steamed, boiled or sautéed as with other green vegetables. An infusion made from the leaves may be used as a cough remedy.

Precautions: The plant is quite resilient and will retain any chemical that it has been sprayed with, so be sure to forage for this plant in places where it has not be chemically sprayed or treated.

CONCLUSION

Throughout the pages of this book, we have thoroughly discussed a compendium of the most common edible wild plants throughout North America and the steps on how you can make the most of their edible parts. We have discussed the best times to forage for these plants and the suggested preparations that you can do for specific parts, though you are definitely free to experiment to see which dishes best complement their unique flavors. In earlier chapters too, we have discussed on how you can easily preserve the bounty that you have foraged from nature and the steps on how to ensure your continued safety as you forage for more edible wild plants. The book also discussed our role in the continuation of our stewardship over the earth, and how it is our responsibility to ensure that others are able to enjoy the fruits of the soil in the same way we do.

Keep your eyes peeled, and your mind open as the plant that you may despise in your gardens may become the food source of your future. All it takes it is the necessary knowledge that you need to ensure that you are able to safely harvest the plants that you can safely consume.

9 781915 331380